IN HIS PRESENCE
A Book on Liturgy and Prayer

Eugene O'Sullivan, O.P.

Michael Glazier, Inc.
Wilmington, Delaware

First published in 1980 by
Michael Glazier Inc., 1210 King Street,
Wilmington, DE 19801

and

Dominican Publications
Upper Dorset Street
St. Saviour's
Dublin 1, Ireland

Library of Congress Catalog Card No: 80-68396
ISBN (Michael Glazier Inc.): 0-89453-184-0
ISBN (Dominican Publications): 0-097271-01-4

Design & Typography by Robert Zerbe Graphics

Cover design by Lillian Brulc

Printed in the United States of America

I will let him come freely into my
presence and he can come close to me;
who else, indeed, would risk his life
by coming close to me – it is the Lord
who speaks.

Jer. 30:21

Contents

1 STILLNESS

LITURGY, at its heart, is not something that we do. The best clue to the nature of liturgy is given by Isaiah:

> "In all their affliction he was afflicted, and the angel of his presence saved them; in his love and in his pity he redeemed them; he lifted them up and carried them all the days of old." (63:9)

It is his presence that heals us. All of liturgy is about coming into the presence of God, and being healed. That presence is experienced in various ways in the liturgy, and as we open ourselves to it, it forms us. Liturgy is first about being in the presence of the redeeming Lord, being healed by his presence; and therefore, liturgy is something that he does to us rather than things we do in response. As you cannot have a "royal occasion" unless a king or queen agrees to be present, liturgy is possible only because God has called us into his presence. Of course, our response is important, but it is a trap to equate liturgy without activity.

Romano Guardini's comments on Stillness in *Meditations Before Mass*[1] seem to be the most important introduction to any study of liturgy.

---

[1]Meditations Before Mass by Romano Guardini, pp.3-15 (Newman Press, 1955)

"If someone were to ask me what the liturgical life begins with, I should answer: with learning stillness. Without it, everything remains superficial vain. Our understanding of stillness is nothing strange or aesthetic. Were we to approach stillness on the level of aesthetics – of mere withdrawal into the ego – we should spoil everything. What we are striving for is something very grave, very important, and unfortunately, sorely neglected; the prerequisite of the liturgical holy act.

Stillness is the tranquility of the inner life; the quiet at the depths of its hidden stream. It is a collected, total presence, a being 'all there,' receptive, alert, ready. There is nothing inert or oppressive about it.

Attentiveness – that is the clue to the stillness in question, the stillness before God."

Guardini's point on the need for silence is still crucial and, I should think, it is still the most neglected part of liturgy.

In the liturgy we are being healed by being "allowed to stand in your presence" (Eucharistic Prayer II). Silence and stillness are the prerequisite, and also man's first response to that presence. For many people, to take silence seriously will demand a change in their whole spiritual outlook. It means first, that one must not think of forgiveness or the service of God in terms of one's own activities, even the activities of praying and singing. It is his presence that heals us, and therefore, we need to learn to be still, to be open, to be receptive in his presence.

Most of us have learned a great deal about liturgy and participation over the last twenty years. In 1958, the Decree of Pope Pius XII on Music and Liturgy gave great encouragement to active participation, especially through singing. In particular, Pius XII recommended what came to be called the "Four Hymn Mass." It really originated in Germany during the Nazi period, when the only time that a priest could speak to his people was during the Mass. And there, in the 1930's, under that pressure, priests devised this style of Mass, with much vernacular singing, as a way of communicating the message of Christ as effectively as possible within the hour allowed. The Four Hymn Mass, or as it was known at that time "the German Mass," became the model for participation.

From 1964 onwards the Decrees of the Council were published. However, some misunderstanding arose, because most of us tended to interpret the Council's statements in terms of the 1958 Decree, of six years earlier. We did not notice that the Council was putting forward a new and different understanding of the theology of liturgy, and so also, by implication, a different outlook on spirituality, and new approaches to prayer. For a number of years we continued to think of participation in terms of more singing, more talking, more acting together, that is, in terms of the 1958 Decree. There is no point in feeling guilty about it; all of us somewhat missed many of the nuances at first. Growth and reform are always slow processes.

It is only now, when some of the silt is beginning to settle, that we can return once more to catch further insight through re-reading the Council's Constitution on the Liturgy, especially that great paragraph 7.

> ". . . Christ is always present in his Church, especially in her liturgical celebrations. He is present in the Sacrifice of the Mass not only in the person of his minister, "the same now offering, through the ministry of priests, who formerly offered himself on the cross," but especially in the eucharistic species. By his power he is present in the sacraments so that when anybody baptizes it is really Christ himself who baptizes. He is present in his word since it is he himself who speaks when the holy scriptures are read in the Church. Lastly, he is present when the Church prays and sings, for he has promised "where two or three are gathered together in my name there am I in the midst of them" (Mt 18:20).
>
> "Christ, indeed, always associates the Church with himself in this great work in which God is perfectly glorified and men are sanctified. The Church is his

beloved Bride who calls to her Lord, and through him offers worship to the eternal Father.

"The liturgy, then, is rightly seen as an exercise of the priestly office of Jesus Christ. It involves the presentation of man's sanctification under the guise of signs perceptible by the senses and its accomplishment in ways appropriate to each of these signs. In it full public worship is performed by the Mystical Body of Jesus Christ, that is, by the Head and his members.

"From this it follows that every liturgical celebration, because it is an action of Christ the Priest and of his Body, which is the Church, is a sacred action surpassing all others. No other action of the Church can equal its efficacy by the same title and to the same degree."

We can now recognise what wonderful insight on prayer is contained in this paragraph. We can recognise too that although the practical changes in the rubrics which resulted are quite significant, if the truth must be told, they are secondary. It is quite secondary whether the priest says Mass facing you, or with his back to you, in comparison to the new understanding of the sacraments that emerged from the Council:

Christ is present in the liturgy in four ways – in the priest presiding, the people gathered, the Word read, and the sacred meal shared. In the light of Isaiah's remark we must come to a new understanding of that presence in Christ.

Christ is present in this priest presiding, healing us.

Christ is present in the words of scripture read to us, healing us.

Christ is present in this meal of bread and wine.

Christ is present in all of us here, and through our gathering, healing us. (Perhaps this is the most neglected feature.)

Since the Council, we have been beneficially occupied in attempting to put these Decrees into practice. But there is some validity in the objection one hears that, in our enthusiasm for changing the furniture and getting everyone to join in the prayers, we have, to some degree, lost prayer. It is true that as we moved beyond the suggestions about singing, in the 1958 Decree, and tried to make paragraph 7 a concrete reality, stressing the four symbols, as we have tried our best to emphasise the importance of the altar, the priest's chair and the lectern, we did not grasp sufficiently their meaning. It is much easier to change the furniture than to change one's way of thinking. It is much easier to change the rubrics and the various actions which the priest does, than to change our way of praying. Yet nothing less than that was being asked of us: a change in our way of praying, gradual as this of necessity must be.

The people gathered, the priest presiding, the Word read, the sacred meal shared, are all ways in which Christ's presence is experienced, and is conveyed to us. To this, our first response must be one of silence, of stillness, of attentiveness and receptivity, in order that that presence may form us. The Mass is the point at which it is possible for the Christian to be most deeply drawn into the mystery of God, the mystery of Christ in us, drawn into the presence. In the words of Vincent Ferrer: "The Mass is the highest act of contemplation." As Eucharistic Prayer II says, just after the consecration, "we thank you for allowing us to stand in your presence and serve you." "To be in the presence" is the heart of liturgy. It is what prayer and contemplativeness are about. To be formed by that presence is what Christian life is about.

Being a Christian means being drawn into the holiness of Christ, the holiness of God, and thereby having one's activity and one's mentality changed. St. Paul's letter to the Colossians shows how he dealt with people at such a spiritual transition point. St. Paul was speaking to fairly new converts, many of them of Jewish background, who were trying to adapt to a new spirituality, a new way of praying. It seemed to them that just learning to live in the presence of Christ, as the heart of Christian spirituality, without all the external beauty and spectacle of the Jewish

ritual, to which they were accustomed, was dull and drab –
a very impoverished sort of thing. They got weary of it.
The same problem turns up later, in the Letter to the
Hebrews. The "Hebrews" were probably convert Jewish
priests, also trying to make that transition into a new way
of praying. By comparison, they too found Christian prayer
became wearisome. As with the Colossians, Paul had to
bring these people to learn new ways of praying, but above
all, to learn not to lose prayer in the transition.

> "Let us fix our eyes on Jesus, the origin and the crown
> of all faith, who, to win his prize of blessedness, endured
> the cross and made light of its shame, Jesus, who now
> sits on the right of God's throne. Take your standard
> from him, from his endurance, from the enmity the
> wicked bore him, and you will not grow faint, you will not
> find your souls unmanned." (Hebrews 12:2-3)

We ourselves are in much the same situation. Most of us
remember the days of the Latin Mass, we remember the
stillness, we remember its prayerfulness, even when we did
not understand all that was being said, and could not hear
most of it. It would be a great pity if, at this stage, we could
not find again a point of contact with that prayerfulness
and so draw back into our present liturgy that quality of
contemplativeness. Liturgy is about that stillness of a man
before God, in the presence of God, the stillness in "the
presence that heals us," heals our vision, heals the various
wounds which our sins, and others, have inflicted on us.
But to be healed, we do have to learn again to be still.

Two obvious practical implications arise from what has
been said.

1. When we come to liturgy, both to participating in it
   ourselves, or in planning it for others, we must give
   due importance to silence. We have to resist the
   inclination to fill every gap with chatter or singing.

2. There must be stillness in sound, and also a kind of
   visual silence. That means, for example, that when
   the priest begins to say the Opening Collect (or whenever he is praying aloud) he must not be visually inter-
   rupted by someone walking up the aisle with a collection plate, or a reader coming to the lectern. Only
   one thing must happen at a time. Whatever is done
   must be allowed to have its full impact, and must not
   be disrupted. That is part of the stillness we need, the
   stillness that enables a person to hear the Word in
   order to be formed by it.

Along with Guardini's chapter on Stillness, I also recommend Guardini's Letter to the Mainz Conference in 1964,
with the special emphasis it gives to "participation through
looking." Once again, I think we have to learn what for most
of us is a totally new technique in prayer. In our childhood
closing our eyes and saying our prayers were almost equivalent terms. You closed your eyes at prayers, mainly to
exclude distraction. Even at Mass we either read the missal,
or closed our eyes. So, even now, when the priest holds up
the host before communion and says "Behold the Lamb of
God," every head bends down, and no-one looks. We are
quite unused to the idea that looking is one of the most
basic ways of participating in the liturgy. It is one of the
simplest and oldest ways of praying. The story is told of
the Cure of Ars when he noticed an old man who spent long
periods in the church, apparently doing nothing, the saint
asked him what he did all this time, and he replied simply
"I look at him, and he looks at me."

The comments of Guardini are worth noting:

"The basic question then is this: of what does the inte-
grated liturgical act consist?

"This becomes clearest when it is a matter of 'doing,' for
instance, the offertory procession, where this is customary.
It makes all the difference whether the faithful look on this
procession as a mere means to an end which could have been
achieved equally well by someone coming round with the

collection-plate, or whether they know that the act of bringing their gifts is a 'prayer' in itself, a readiness towards God.

"The act of 'doing' can also incorporate a thing, in this case a coin; or holy water for the sign of the cross; and the celebrant has the bread and the chalice with the wine. There is no need for words to give the 'meaning,' for it is realized in the act itself. The same is true of localities and special places, times, days and hours.

"The liturgical act can be realized by looking. This does not merely mean that the sense of vision takes note of what is going on in front, but it is in itself a living participation in the act. I once experienced this in Palermo Cathedral when I could sense the attention with which the people were following the blessings on Holy Saturday for hours on end without books or any words of 'explanation.' Much of this was, of course, an external 'gazing,' but basically it was far more. The looking by the people was an act in itself; by looking they participated in the various actions. However, cinema, radio and television – not to forget the flood of tourists – will have destroyed this remainder of old contemplative forces.

"Only if regarded in this way can the liturgical-symbolical action be properly understood: for instance, the washing of hands by the celebrant, but also liturgical gestures like the stretching out of hands over the chalice. It should not be necessary to have to add in words of thought, 'this means such and such,' but the symbol should be 'done' by the celebrant as a religious act and the faithful should 'read' it by an analogous act; they should see the inner sense in the outward sign. Without this everything would be a waste of time and energy and it would be better simply to 'say' what was meant. But the 'symbol' is in itself something corporal-spiritual, an expression of the inward through the outward, and must as such be co-performed through the act of looking."

There is a noticeable contrast between the reaction of an audience at a lecture, where everyone instinctively looks at the speaker, and the same group of people celebrating Mass together, where it would require a distinct effort to get the congregation to look at the priest. From our earliest days we have been trained to think that the first requirement for saying our prayers was to close our eyes. This is why I say that it is necessary for us to learn a new technique of prayer, especially with regard to the sacraments. Part of the force and effectiveness of a sacrament, or of any symbol or ritual, is that it has to be seen, so that it may be experienced, it becomes the vehicle by which Christ's presence is known. A general principle underlying many of the reforms of recent years is that "the sacred symbols in the liturgy are to be experienced as intensely as possible." This means, for example, you cannot really hear the Word of God if it is poorly read – it cannot affect you as a sacrament. One may make up for it by one's devotion and personal prayer, but the actual sacramental effect is almost totally disrupted. In the same way, part of the sign, or the symbol, of the priest preaching or presiding, is that he speaks to you, that you and he have contact, eye to eye, with each other. It is through this personal contact that the call of Christ comes to you individually. In the same way, the bread and wine of the Eucharistic meal are something to be looked at; and for the rest of the day it is through the memory of what we have seen and eaten that we live on in Christ's presence. After the Mass we must carry with us the presence into which we have been brought; and it is still through the symbols and signs of the Eucharist, the bread and wine remembered, that that presence is both called to mind, and its effectiveness continued. We must learn to look; learn to be still.

Learning to listen and learning to look, lead to the two most common forms of Christian prayer. In this context it is very handy for us to use the language used by Eastern mystics, and Eastern methods of meditation (such as transcendental meditation, yoga), namely, the two terms: mantra and mandalla. In Eastern meditation methods a mantra is simply a single word or sound or phrase which is repeated over and over; repeated interiorly. In fact, the practice is exactly parallel to the method of prayer recommended in most of the Christian writings on prayer (e.g. *The Cloud of Unknowing*). It is the practice the Jews used as well. When the Gospel says of our Lady, that "she kept all these things, pondering on them in her heart," it means that Mary repeated those words over and over again: "behold the handmaid of the Lord," . . . "behold the handmaid of the Lord." In all early Christian monastic writing, to "teach prayer" meant simply to teach the psalms – to teach someone to take a line of the psalm and allow it to turn over and over within. Sometimes a line like "into your hands I commend my spirit," simplified itself down, perhaps into a syllable or two – "your hands" – which captures the whole prayer. The repeated use of the word "Father," or "Abba," has the longest tradition of all Christian prayers. One repeated the word, again and again; one allowed the phrase or the word to be repeated interiorly, to echo inside. By this, as one repeats that word, one becomes open to the presence of the Father; all we know of the Father is encapsulated for us in that word, and the Father's presence moulds us. Each of us should try to fix on some single word, or phrase, in the readings in the Mass, and carry it with us throughout the whole day. It has always been through the use of such a technique that Christians have learned to live in the presence of God.

The second term used by the Eastern writers on prayers is the word "mandalla." It usually refers to a picture or even an abstract design. The commonest example of a mandalla familiar to us in the West is the Japanese flower arrangement. The purpose of Japanese flower arrangements is not just to brighten up a dark corner of the room, or to make the room look pretty. It is essentially to do with meditation – with Zen meditation. The flower arrangement is to be looked at, to be contemplated. The Japanese garden is similar. Other mandallas are simple pictorial patterns. One contemplates it, and in contemplating, one begins to penetrate the meaning of our existence, of being.

The obvious parallel in the Christian world is the Cross; the Cross is the Christian mandalla. All of us have learned to look at it, without words. It seems, as a general rule, that the deeper one's prayer, the fewer words one will use, the more one will just sit and look. Looking silently at the Cross has always been one of the great Christian methods of praying, especially in time of suffering or in time of grief. It does not need any words. The confused bewilderment of our minds in the face of sorrow sees that no other explanation could be needed.

But, even more important than the Cross as the Christian mandalla, are the bread and wine, the water, and the oil or perfume. The seven sacraments, and the materials and actions they use, are the most important Christian mandallas. At these we must learn to look, until our gaze is drawn into them, and in them Christ reveals his presence.

A further qualification should be added, that the sacraments, as mandallas, are not objects, like bread and wine, but actions which use these materials. The Christian symbol of using oil is in fact basically a caress, a hug; a hug, with perfume added. A recent writer, speaking about the new Rite of Reconciliation, says that the basic image is that of "being hugged by God." The action of the priest of putting his hand on the head of the penitent, in the Rite of Reconciliation, is the residue of what was originally a hug. So also, in the other sacraments which use an imposition of hands – confirmation, the anointing of the sick, ordination. In each of these the main symbol is the hug. Imposing one's hands on the man being ordained is not the equivalent of royalty dubbing a knight, by placing the sword on his shoulders.

It is not a matter of conferring power or authority. The symbol in each of these sacraments is the hug, by which one is drawn into the love of God; and it is that love that empowers us.

These various actions used in the sacraments are the great Christian mandallas; they are the images, the symbols, the sacraments, in which Christ's presence is experienced. If that experience is to grow, you have to spend time sitting in the presence of that particular sacramental symbol. Sacraments are the material means by which Christ, who died and is risen, is present to us, enlightening us, forming us, drawing us into his life.

The old tradition of spending time "in thanksgiving" after communion was spiritually very sound. It is important to revive that old tradition of spending time in reflection after celebrating any sacrament – not necessarily saying prayers of thanksgiving, but bringing back to memory the bread and wine that you have taken, that you have eaten and drunk, and, in thought, sitting there in the wonder of it, until it can mould you, until it becomes effectively for you the means by which the Lord abides in you, and you in him. In other words, to be effectively a sacrament for you.

Many of the practices neglected in recent years need to be rediscovered. In the years of the change-over the meaning or the value of some of these, for example, thanksgiving after communion, was not seen very well. The argument one usually heard over those years was that the word "Eucharist" meant "thanksgiving," and therefore, because there cannot be a "thanksgiving for a thanksgiving," it was asserted that at the end of Mass everyone should abruptly stop prayer and get on with the apostolate. It almost became a sign of spiritual cowardice not to leave instantly. Fair enough, thanksgiving may have been the wrong word. But what it represented is utterly indispensable. There must be a time of stillness, when mentally, interiorly, you look at the bread and wine that you have eaten, the symbols you have watched, and in this wordless looking, you allow the Lord to form you. In looking at the bread, all that has been said throughout the whole of Revelation, from Abraham through to the end of the Apocalypse is recalled – the bread that is man's food, the bread that was the manna in the desert, the bread which strengthened Elijah on his journey to Sinai, the bread which, when we eat, we take the body of the Lord, and proclaim his death and resurrection until he comes. All this is recaptured, without any word, in looking at the bread and wine. Christ is present in these sacred signs. But if we are not willing to remain for some time during the day living in the memory of those sacramental signs and in the consciousness of that presence, the sacrament is rendered largely fruitless.

Liturgy, as I say, is not first about our singing hymns, or our reading prayers of the faithful, or about our bringing up the gifts. It is first about the presence of Christ, that presence that heals us.

Let us return once more to paragraph 7 of the Constitution: Christ is present in the liturgy, in the congregation gathered, in the priest presiding, in the scripture read, and in the sacred meal shared.

As a result of this basic principle, there are a number of practical consequences which find expression even in the architecture of a church, and in the lay-out of the sanctuary. In the sanctuary there are just three pieces of furniture – there is the chair for the priest presiding, there is the lectern, the table of the Word, and then, the altar, the table of the Eucharist. Here in the sanctuary too, we need another kind of visual stillness, the sense of quietness which is produced by the absence of unnecessary furniture. Not only is it not correct to have statues in the sanctuary, other than the Cross, we need to remove also all unnecessary extra chairs, kneelers and little tables, all of which detract from the powerful symbolism of one chair, from which the priest presides, one table, at which the Eucharist is celebrated, one table or lectern for the bible or lectionary.

If then the priest is to be seen as presiding, the chair must be placed in such a way that he can actually see, that he can communicate with his eyes as well as with his voice.

He must not disappear behind the altar when he sits down. Furthermore, the priest must not be too far back from the people, and remote from the reader. Think of what is said about the priest's relationship to the congregation, and his relationship to the person who is reading, if his chair is too far away. It seems to imply that the readings are something that the people need, but that they do not concern the priest. He is not seen to be part of the Church listening to the Word of God. The priest too must be a listener to the Word of God, and he must be seen to be a listener to the Word. Visually, it must be obvious to the congregation that the priest is listening to the Word, with them; the Word which calls both him and them to faith. In listening, he is one with the people to whom God speaks.

That, of course, brings out the need for other readers, and the total inappropriateness of either the priest doing all the readings, or the priest not being seen to be the listener. Normally, in fact, if there is another priest present, or a deacon, the celebrant is not supposed to read the Gospel. He must listen. His two main functions, as the one who presides, are to preach the homily and to recite the Eucharistic prayer.

So, during the readings, the priest presides by being seen to be a listener to the Word of God, and, as it were, saying "If it is worthwhile for me to listen to this, you will find it worthwhile also." Most of our human values are shared in such a way. If a significant person thinks that something is important, then others will tend to think so as well. That is the way in which children absorb most of their parents' values or their teachers' values. Since then, the priest presides at the liturgy of the Word by being seen to be a listener, it is imperative that he can be seen.

A similar point must be made about the lectern. There must be good relative proportion between the size of these three pieces of furniture in the sanctuary. To have an enormously large altar, with a kitchen chair at one side and a music stand at the other, makes an unbalanced theological statement. And it is well to remember that it is making a theological statement.

Lastly, it is necessary to stress that these three objects ought to be permanently in place. It is still not uncommon, after the reading, for someone to pop out and cart the lectern and lectionary off into a corner. The lectern is meant to be a permanent symbol. In fact, it is good if the book could be there at all times, so that, when the liturgy is not being celebrated, it may be read by anyone who wishes to meditate on it. The table of the Word needs permanence and dignity, like the altar and the chair. And none of them should dwarf the others.

Since the Renaissance, it has become customary to have very long altars. But in the ancient Basilica at Ravenna, from the 6th century, the altar is about 2½ feet long and 1½ feet wide. All it needed to carry was the chalice and the bread. I am not demanding that this is what we should now do; but it is a fairly good precedent. The custom of having a very long altar against the wall developed in the 16th century at the time when great paintings were placed above the altar, on the back wall of the sanctuary. For architectural reasons then, the altar was elongated, to act as a plinth on which, visually, the painting stood. That very secular circumstance is the origin of our 15 feet long altars.

Although I have spoken about the pieces of furniture, the task of decluttering the sanctuary must never allow us to be distracted from the presence that is expressed and experienced there, signalled to us through those three pieces of furniture – Christ the risen Lord, enlightening our minds in the Word, the Eucharistic meal and the priest presiding. The sanctuary must contain these three. Other things, such as candles and flowers, banners and other works of art, have their place, and when used with sensitivity and discretion they do have an important part to play. But their's is essentially the task of enhancing our experience of Christ's presence in the Word, the sacred meal, the priest, the people. They highlight the power of the symbols.

Listening to the Word spoken has one other major factor
working against it in the new lectionary, that there are
altogether too many words, too much talking. Perhaps
more correctly, there are too many unconnected pieces of text
to be got through, most of which are unrelated to the other
bits: three readings, responses, antiphons.

Strangely enough, in regard to the first reading, the
greatest difficulty arises from the fact that it is usually too
short to be able to convey its sense, and it is so out of context
that it usually sounds quite indistinguishable from the bits
of exhortation which we had last Sunday and will get again
next Sunday too. Chapter 8 will deal more fully with this
problem. However, let me offer one generalisation to keep
in mind; you do not cure boredom by shortening it. People
can sit happily and enjoy a story from the Old Testament
which takes three or four minutes to tell; but no-one would
believe it if they were told that many of the passages which
they consider boring actually are so short that they last no
more than fifty seconds (Try timing them.)

The general impression of an unrelenting torrent of words
is not helped by the fact that many priests say all the prayers
aloud, even those which are forbidden to be said aloud.
No matter how nice the prayers may be, the endless drone
of the priest's voice will inevitably kill all the poetry and
fervour. But not only this: sacred silence is something of
immense importance in its own right, and it is wrong to
deprive the people of the silence, when the rubrics explicitly
prescribe it.

Finally, to sum up:

1. Learn to listen, allow yourself to be formed by the
   readings. The liturgy of the Word is a sacrament; Christ
   is really present, calling you to faith, healing you.
2. Learn to look, and learn to live on throughout the day,
   in the memory of what you have seen and heard. The
   basic Christian prayer of living in the presence of God
   needs a focus. For the Christian, the focus of such a
   prayer is either the Word of God spoken to us in the

liturgy, or the sacred symbols which we have watched, in which we have participated.

> "Something which has existed since the beginning,
>   that we have heard,
>   and we have seen with our own eyes;
>   that we have watched
>   and touched with our hands:
>   the Word, who is life –
>   this is our subject." (1 John 1:1)

Looking is important throughout the Mass, but especially as you come to communion. Take the host in your hand, and do not move away until you have had time to look at it and then eat it. This moment is much too precious in the life of the individual Christian for it to be rushed by traffic rules about stepping aside, and getting out of people's way; it must not be subordinated to consideration about getting everyone out of the church in fifty minutes in order to clear the car-park. If it is felt that communion has to be given more quickly in any church the answer is to use more special ministers. No-one should feel rushed at communion. In this regard it may be necessary to devise some manner of coming to communion other than forming long queues. The presence of a queue at one's back inevitably makes a person feel under pressure to rush. One should give oneself time to experience the eating and the drinking, the being nourished, which is the sacramental symbol of the Eucharist.

The response to the presence of God is best expressed in the words of St. John: "The Lamb then broke the seventh seal, and there was silence in heaven for about half an hour." (Apoc 8:1)

2 RE-ASSESSING THE ENTRANCE RITE

THIS CHAPTER might best be described by comparing it to that task which faces you every year when you come home from holidays to find the garden over-grown with weeds, half the vegetables gone to seed and some unidentifiable insect chewing the rose bushes back to their roots. I want to evoke a mild dissatisfaction with what we have been taking for granted in our way of celebrating the Mass in recent years.

There is, of course, lots of dissatisfaction there already, and a great number of people have their own strong views on what to do about it. By and large, most of them are the sort of argument that says "I don't know anything about it, but I know what I like"; "I don't know anything about liturgy but I know what it should be." And on this incontrovertible principle we are slumping more and more into what could be called "liturgy-by-democratic vote." Or, like Alice-in-Wonderland for whom "words mean what I choose them to mean," liturgy comes to mean what I choose it to mean, or whatever the most forceful character in the neighbourhood decides.

The one point on which no one seems willing to give ground is that there might be very clear principles by which good or bad liturgy can be judged, or principles indicating how good liturgy is to be constructed. By that, I am not here referring to Church law on the subject, but to something more basic than Church law, something which derives from the nature of sacraments or ritual, whether it be a baptism, a funeral, or a Mass or any other sacrament or sacramental rite.

Time and again one is confronted with the undisguised resentment which states that "you have no right to lay down the law as to how we are going to participate," or "people are used to this now, and you should stop interfering; they have as much right as you to decide how they will do things."

Out of this mentality, types of religious services are developing which may be quite reverent, but which have almost exactly the same relationship to the sacrament as had the old practice of forty years ago of saying the Rosary out loud during the entire Mass. It is excellent that people should pray while Mass is going on, but that is not all that the Church asks, especially in the Constitution on the Liturgy. It is excellent that people should be catechised, to understand their faith better, but the 1977 Synod has made it emphatically clear that the Mass is not only about catechising. The Synod made the point quite clear that viewing the liturgy merely as a catechetical tool would be an aberration.

Not infrequently a side-show of one kind or another is being offered as an alternative focus of attention. It may be a commentator, or a teacher explaining things, or a local music group waiting in the wings for the next gap in the proceedings in order to "render another item," or it may be something which is really an unrelated para-liturgy. No matter how prayerful or instructive all this may be, it is not participation in the liturgy. And it is the liturgy, especially the Mass, that is the "primary and indispensable source of the true Christian spirit" (Pius X). There is a very fine and delicate line to be drawn here, but more often than not, the distortion in any particular case derives from an over-emphasis on an element which is perhaps of some importance, but still is only secondary. Any elaboration of the rite for catechetical purposes, or to enable some particular group to participate, needs to be built on the central symbol of the particular sacrament.

For example, the essential sign in baptism is that of being buried in water, of going down into the grave with Christ, and coming up again. Baptism is like the passage through the Red Sea, the passage into death's valley, or the passage through the Jordan, through the grave to resurrection. Going into the water expresses how one puts one's life into the hands of God, and it is he who gives it back transformed.

This core symbol is well illustrated by the plan devised in one parish. After the priest had explained the meaning of baptism, an increasing number of parents had asked to have their babies baptised by immersion. It therefore became necessary to find a suitable baptismal font. The parish is not in a well-off suburb, but it has more than its quota of good artists (since artists are usually not wealthy). They used a perspex hospital basinette, framed in local wood, with beaten copper panels, allowing about eight inches of water visible at each side. A local potter helped the children of the parish to throw a large water-pitcher. The water being poured into the baptistry, gurgling from the mouth of the jar, announces its own presence, it is there living and plentiful. After the blessing of the font, at the renewal of baptismal vows, each of the parents and god-parents comes forward, puts his or her hand right into the water, and signs himself with the words "this is our faith, this is the faith of the Church. I pledge myself to Christ Jesus our Lord." This allows each one to experience, at least to some extent, what it is like to go into the water, into the grave with Christ, and to come up again. This small gesture evokes a sense of being involved in ritual of extraordinary force, as the baby is then baptised by immersion. Here we are using the precisely accurate symbol, and it speaks to everyone powerfully.

Quenching thirst, which is such an obvious way of thinking about water, is therefore not the primary symbolism. Likewise, the primary symbolism is not about being washed in water, but rather being buried. True enough there is scriptural basis for these secondary layers of meaning, and since they seem simpler to grasp, it is not surprising that often they are made central. Like the baths in Lourdes, the primary symbolism of water in baptism needs hardly any explanation, if given a chance. As in Lourdes, it is not just the coldness of the water that is stunning, but the stark vividness of the symbolism as one is lowered, helplessly, into the pool, one's life is in the hands of the attendants, and, through that, one's life is entrusted to God.

Unfortunately, I suspect that many inappropriate practices have crept into parish churches from school Masses. I know that even mentioning this will be taken to be almost equivalent to an attack on motherhood, but a predominant danger in the liturgy is that of aiming everything at children. Yet one must insist, whether to teachers or to parents, that adults need to spend the major part of the time they give to prayer in contact with other adults, with others who are spiritually involved in the same kind of faith-and-prayer stage of development as themselves. A husband and wife need to pray together on their own, apart from the family prayers they say with the children. Apart from prayer on one's own, singly, each of us needs to pray in the company of others who share our kind of life, our stage of development in life. A man in his forties and a priest in his forties share almost completely the same kinds of spiritual problems, spiritual points of development. It is essential that we, as adults, pray together. No matter how different our lives may be on the surface, we go through the same struggles, and God does not mitigate the pain because of our vocation to be priests, or religious, or whatever else we may be.

Quite emphatically, we have to suspend the question "how do we tell this to the children? or how do I put this across to my class tomorrow?" If this preoccupation keeps us from personal involvement in this sacrament, at an adult level, we never will know what it is that we want to pass on to our children.

Western society has a strong child-centered bias. We are in danger therefore, of developing what might be called a "Peter Pan-Catholicism" which is of little use to real children or to real adults. Children are not interested only in the doings of other children. That is why they admire their fathers and mothers. That is why they spend hours marvelling at dad's competence, as he does a botched job repairing a kitchen tap. So, a spirituality of the Baby Jesus has limited appeal even to young children; they do not want to be like a Peter Pan Jesus, who never grows up. In the same way, a spirituality or a liturgy which is always trying to cater for the supposed needs of children leaves the adult community undernourished.

There is a spiritual dishonesty in presenting religion (even to children) as though it were all about the warm cosiness of bedtime stories. Such an approach guarantees also that we will never look to religion for guidance in the real crises of life, let alone consider it as the high point of life. After all, the Jews spent 1800 years in faithful service of God without any idea of life after death or eternal reward or God as a comfortable companion. For them, to serve God was its own reward. They understood what Chesterton meant when he said: "Man is tallest when he bows." One is not coaxed or bribed into a relationship of love with God (the Covenant) like a child being bribed with chocolates. One has to give one's whole self, with the completeness with which God gives himself to us. The greatest image in scripture to convey the meaning of religion, is marriage, the faithful marriage, the adult commitment of man and wife: God's marriage, his covenant with his spouse, Israel, his people. It is blasphemous to imply that religion is like having a playmate at kindergarten. There is a dangerous spiritual dishonesty about making religion insipid, or a matter to do with children, or at least a childish mentality.

This example of religious dishonesty brings me to the three headings used by Ralph Keifer in his article *Squalor On Sunday – Ritual-Imbalance, Ugliness, Dishonesty*.[2]

Ritual Imbalance: This means simply that the various elements of the rite are not in well-balanced proportion, the unimportant things are stealing too much of the limelight.

By now it is standard to think of the Mass as containing two main parts: the liturgy of the Word, and the liturgy of the Eucharist. But at the back of our minds remains the division we remember from the catechism, which said that the three main parts of the Mass are the offertory, the consecration and the priest's communion. There was also the Mass of the Catechumens, or the Fore-Mass, as it was called, but all one had to remember about that was that it was not a sin to miss it. The prayer at the foot of the altar, Kyrie, Gloria, epistle, gospel, sermon, creed, were mere introduction, and expendible.

The reform of the liturgy has changed this radically. The offertory is just not there any longer, it has simply been abolished; and no amount of offertory hymns or offertory processions can bring it back again. On the other hand, the liturgy of the Word has been restored to its original dignity; it is not a relatively unimportant introductory rite. It is, and it always has been, a sacrament, in the strict sense of the term. Christ is present in the liturgy of the Word, acting on us, in exactly the same sense as we say confession is a sacrament in which Christ acts on us. There is a real presence of Christ in the liturgy of the Word.

Well, that is what the new theory says anyhow! In our practice however, we have not yet grasped its implications. Most parishes still have full-blown offertory processions and hymns. In practice, most parishes have elongated entrance rites: entrance hymns and processions, and probably more singing and activity in the first ten minutes

[2]Worship (May 1970)

of the Mass than in the rest of the Mass put together. In practice, in Ralph Keifer's words, we constantly "accentuate the peripheral," giving all our attention to bits without which we could quite happily survive. We set the dinner table exquisitely so that we are too busy to cook the dinner properly.

Now we have to be fair and acknowledge that this is not due to stupidity or bad will, nor is it all our fault. The entrance rite at present is now longer and more complicated than it was in the old Latin Mass. It appears that there was considerable divergence of thought among those who put together the new rite. As a result we now have seven different bits to the entrance rite – hymn, Sign of the Cross, greeting, and perhaps an explanation of the theme, penitential rite, which may or may not be extended quite considerably, Kyrie, Gloria, opening prayer – and often enough, there is a commentator thrown in besides. Ralph Keifer sums it up: "All of this is capped with an opening prayer that opens nothing but rather mercifully draws to a close what is clearly less an introductory rite than a disparate series of devotional exercises."

The Directory for Children's Masses however, provides us with the general rule of thumb concerning all this. It tells us that in a Mass for children, most of these seven elements in the entrance rite may be omitted. It is sufficient to choose one of them, and do it well. This does not authorise us at a normal Sunday or weekday Mass to omit them all, except one. But it makes the point very strongly that only one of them should be given emphasis at any particular Mass, not all seven. Probably we should sing only one of these, except on special occasions, Christmas or a big feast. As a normal Sunday routine we would need to be much more selective in the amount of singing, and the parts we choose to sing.

Similarly, the penitential rite ought not to be extended into a prolonged examination of conscience. The readings, the Gospel, and the sermon are meant to do that for us. The liturgy of the Word probes our consciences and calls us to repentance. On the other hand, the Eucharist is the normal means by which we are freed from sin, for it draws us close to the Lord, and that, by definition, is forgiveness and healing. (Sin essentially is a turning away from God, forgiveness is to be drawn back.) You don't have to have a prolonged penitential rite to make you ready for the Eucharist.

Enlarging, and so emphasising the penitential rite can give the impression that we can attain freedom from sin, so that we can then get on with the Mass without further thought of sin. That is to misunderstand the sacraments radically. The sacraments are about redemption, about sin being taken away and our being healed. The penitential rite at Mass is not a sort of re-entry permit into the society of those who are already totally freed from all sin, who can then get on with being in the presence of God whose company they well suit.

It should be noted too that if phrases are being inserted into the Kyrie they should be acclamations to the Risen Lord. They must not be confessions of sin e.g. "Lord for our sins of injustice, Lord have mercy." The eight sets of examples given in the missal show how they should be phrased. The Kyrie originally had nothing to do with the penitential rite. It is an acclamation to the Risen Lord, into whose presence we come. The Risen Lord shows his mercy and love precisely by being with us.

The highlight of the liturgy of the Word must be the Word. The purpose of the entrance rite is merely to prepare us to hear the Word. It is getting things totally back to front if the entrance rite is so long and so intensely involving that it leaves the congregation exhausted, or agitated, with the result that they slump back into their seats and take a rest during the readings and the sermon.

It is equally unbalanced if the Eucharistic Prayer, which is the great hymn of praise and thanksgiving for creation and redemption, has been anticipated and upstaged by having it all said in the entrance hymn or offertory hymn. Yet, that is the kind of thing we do with the Eucharistic Prayer. Apart from the Words of Institution, it has already been said at much greater length and with much more solemnity in hymns and prayers of the faithful, so that the Eucharistic Prayer is left sounding rather dull, rather repetitive, and not terribly important.

Our main task then, on recognising this kind of ritual imbalance, is to find ways of redressing that balance. How does one go about making a liturgy of the Word which is leisurely, important, formative, prayerful, which is experienced as a call to repentance? That is the task you set yourself when you ask: "How do we enable people to participate in the liturgy of the Word?"

A simple rule of thumb is offered in the directive used in the Archdiocese of Paris. It suggests that one first ask the rather mundane question: how much time have we got for this particular celebration? One can then go on to ask: how much material can be used in that time to best advantage, for this particular congregation? For example, with regard to something like the Easter Vigil, one should first decide how long it is to last. If it is decided that forty-five minutes would be a suitable length for this congregation, one next asks how many of the nine readings available in the lectionary could be fitted in, in a leisurely way, with silences, prayers and some hymns, in that time. There is no question of reciting every possible text. The first objective is to enable this congregation to hear the Word of God. Only a good balance of readings, silence, explanation and prayer can achieve this with profit. And that needs careful planning. One must start with such simple observations as the time it takes to sing a hymn or read a passage of scripture. Ritual imbalance is guaranteed if one starts by choosing four hymns – which will take about sixteen minutes – if the Mass is meant to be ended in thirty-five to forty minutes.

Approach planning then, with this idea of a leisurely liturgy, so that whether you are taking twenty-five to thirty minutes for a weekday Mass, or fifty to sixty minutes or more on a Sunday, you first assess how much can these people take, how much can we celebrate with dignity.

There is, however, one further comment. The ideal is not a twenty minute liturgy. The whole of the Eastern Christian Church – Greek and Russian, Ukranian, Maronite, both Catholic and Orthodox, all take an average of about three hours, even up to five hours, for a Sunday liturgy. Karl Rahner makes the point that he cannot understand how, what it takes three hours for half of Christendom to achieve, can be achieved effectively by the other half in twenty minutes.

Ugliness, like beauty, is too readily assumed to be only in the eye of the beholder. The examples given by Ralph Keifer make it clear that he is dealing with something more basic than mere good taste. Aristotle's statement that beauty, if truth, is the basis for his theory of art. Beauty is a particular kind of truth. In some way, other than its mere verbal content, an object or a line of music expresses some insight into the reality of life or being. Ugliness makes an untrue statement. Yet because it is basically in the area of non-verbal statements it is hard to show that this is not a question of taste, or accustomed use.

When Ralph Keifer gives his example of the ugliness of having two altars in the one sanctuary one cannot reply that two altars could be fitted in with the best of taste. He is speaking of the theological ugliness: the objects are making a wrong statement about God and the meaning of liturgy.

So too, when one objects to bad readers in church it is not principally a complaint about the standards of elocution. If readers cannot be heard, or they just fail to make sense of the readings, and if this goes on week after week, quite clearly the statement is being made that scripture is not worth hearing, and in any case it is largely nonsense. Ugliness is an enacted falsehood.

There is a real need at present for things of beauty in our churches. We have been through a period when many new or restructured churches were as sterile as an operating theatre, with vast, empty, unadorned walls. The interim solution in many places has been to cover the space with children's posters and cartoons. One is visually assaulted as by the most brash of television advertising. It may be best not to argue about this situation; thankfully people are now coming to see that it is inappropriate. At this stage many are ready to welcome things of beauty again. These things refine the soul and alert us to what is wholesome and good, and, even when we do not notice it happening, they alert us to God.

The inadequacy of many church buildings is becoming evident among communities of religious at present. Many religious houses have in the last ten years built or redesigned their chapels. However, for some years now, it has been quite common for a priest to be asked to celebrate Mass in the community room. More recently still, in many convents, sisters are setting aside a room somewhere in the house as a prayer-room. Consider for a moment what all this says. Very obviously the sisters or brothers are not comfortable celebrating Mass in their chapel. The design looked fine on the architect's plan. It would probably be quite all right if its main use was for private meditation, but many of these buildings ignore basic rules of thumb about the dynamics of group activity, and therefore, of liturgy. For example, to form a cohesive group people need to be at least within easy arms-length of the next person, not separated like students in an examination room.

Ask then, what is wrong with the chapel that forces the community to set up another prayer-room? Is it that the chapel, as designed, is not a place conducive to prayer. If that is the case, and I think nearly always it is, then the thing to do is change the chapel. It does not work. And what it is at present doing to the prayerlife of the community might well be very serious. Many new chapels are quite bad: they do not work. Whatever the atmosphere is that is found so good for Mass in the community room, that quality must be brought into the chapel. There is a terrible precedent in this regard. The Temple in Jerusalem had to be destroyed when it became an obstacle to true service of God. Incidentally, even on grounds of Canon Law alone, it is not proper to have Mass like that in any place one feels like.

There is also the question of decor. In this regard it strikes me that why many people find it impossible to pray in some of our redesigned churches and chapels is that the decor, the carpets, the lightfittings, the whole style, is borrowed from the photographs in some flashy *Ideal Home* magazine. Even though a person might not be able to put his finger on it, what is wrong is that the whole thing speaks of the values of affluent materialism, opposite to Christianity. One could no more pray there than in the foyer of the Intercontinental Hotel. Because a place is poor does not mean that it is not beautiful. More often than not, the ugliest, most ungodly things have been bought at very great and unnecessary expense.

To a lesser extent, all this is applicable also to parish churches. There is something wrong with the design of a church which has to have, what has now come to be taken for granted, a weekday chapel, leaving aside consideration of vast European cathedrals. The average church which seats four to five hundred should not need a second chapel for small groups.

A Blessed Sacrament chapel is quite a different concept, and it is not normally to be assumed that daily Mass will be celebrated there. The early Christian practice, still observed by all the churches of the Eastern Rite, is that any church should have only one altar.

When I speak of ugliness, I am also thinking of some of the lost beauty of our religious heritage – old prayers. Few under twenty would know the *En ego* or the *Anima Christi*. They would know none of the great medieval prayers commonly known twenty years ago, although now forgotten.

Ugliness can often be experienced in the sense of impoverishment which burdens us from time to time, from having lost so many things of beauty in traditional prayers and devotions. Even though the devotions to various saints may have been deficient in one way or other, and most of their plaster statues were lamentably poor art, the celebration of their feasts from day to day did give us a sense of privilege, of having been allowed to rub shoulders with greatness. To have lost that is indeed an impoverishment.

The third element which Ralph Keifer mentioned is dishonesty. We have already dealt with the mistake of always aiming the liturgy at children. Keifer also mentions the dishonesty of false enthusiasm, especially the assumption that "community" implies exuberant demonstrations of affection to people never seen before. Christian community is not about that kind of chumminess. We can validly express such deep affection with very few people. A more casual acquaintance is possible with a larger group. But there is no hope, it is only a pretence, to suggest that we are on that level of intimacy with everyone around us in church on a Sunday morning.

However, there is no doubt that we are aware that all of us are here because we believe in Jesus, because we hope. Each of us knows that he will come again. We know that death is a dimension of the life of every one of us, and, in my dying hours, these people are going to be the people who will be with me, who will pray for me, who will look after those whom I can no longer care for. We are all going on that pilgrimage together, within arm's reach. The sign of peace does not primarily express the fact that we are all one big happy community, because we are not; it would be dishonest to pretend that this is so.

What unites us as we gather for Mass, most of us almost unknown to each other is, first, our faith. We all believe in Christ, in his death and resurrection. We are all following him, hesitantly, walking in darkness, but we stretch out a hand in the dark at times to touch another hand – it assures us that we are still moving in the right direction. The journey is made possible because we know that we do not travel alone.

That touch of a finger in the dark, expresses the delicacy of our contact, our support, of our common trust in the power of Christ leading us.

It would destroy all ability to share our faith more fully, or more explicitly, with other individuals, if we put on an exuberant front of being chummy, and back-slapping. It is phoney and dishonest to give the impression that the Christian agape – the gathering of love – the love feast – the earliest name of the Mass, resembles anything so crude.

Only people who are capable of delicacy can express genuine exuberance, when it is time for that also.

These three characteristic faults – ritual imbalance, ugliness, dishonesty – can be found in most parts of ritual, but it is especially useful to keep them in mind when assessing the entrance rite. However, one further source of trouble needs to be exposed. What seems to motivate so much of the "hard work" put into the entrance rite at ordinary parish Masses is a strong sense that the congregation is far from ready to celebrate the Mass. Somehow it is felt that they must be kept at the door as long as possible, to brush off the dust and clean them up for God. There seems to be an assumption that people urgently need remedial therapy before it would be possible for them to cope with the serious religious reality which is the Mass.

There is therefore, the tendency to sweeten it all, dishing up insipid ditties and tunes, for fear that the real God would frighten them away.

Equally, there is the inclination to load on great screeds of explanation, on the assumption that these people do not really know what they are coming for.

There is the universal urge to elaborate the penitential rite into a heart-searching examination of conscience, out of the fear that the congregation is not really fit to be here.

These three temptations need to be resisted firmly. God can use his own sacraments effectively; the liturgy of the Word and the liturgy of the Eucharist can achieve the work God has sent them to do. The entrance rite is a preparation, and only a preparation. Its purpose is simply to lead the congregation "to be all there, alert, attentive, receptive, ready."

I think that it is because we lack faith in the power of God to use his own sacraments that we keep everyone so long on the threshold that they are exhausted before God gets a chance to have a go at them.

3 SACRAMENTS, RITUALS AND SYMBOLS

IN OUR EVERYDAY SPEECH we use many words loosely, so that the exact meaning of each becomes unclear. Words are often coloured because of associations in one's mind with vaguely similar ideas. Discovering again the meaning of the words we use is the first step in any study, even in religion or theology. Half the questions in the catechism were simply definitions of words. In any serious discussion one has to agree to use a word only in its precise sense.

Often an ordinary dictionary will give us enough information to help distinguish groups of words which we commonly use as though they were not only vaguely similar but interchangeable.

Some such words which concern us here are: ritual, pageantry, rite, drama, or dramatic presentation, symbol or symbolic, sacrament, liturgy, signs.

To begin with, many people tend to confuse ritual, pageantry and drama.

A pageant is a spectacle which uses costumes and brilliant display in order to present a composite picture of some historical period or incident or institution, usually by means of processions or tableaux or scenes depicted in mime. At a simple level, the Nativity play at Christmas in the parish school falls into the category of a pageant.

Drama, by contrast, depends less on spectacle or costume, although it may use them. Drama unfolds a story or an incident in such a way that the audience is drawn into the argument and into the emotional struggles of the characters in the play. The human experiences of joy, fear, love, and the rest are evoked in the audience, and these emotions are purified or understood a little better as one identifies with the characters on the stage.

Ritual is not primarily concerned with historical events presented either in pageant or in dramatic presentation. The Passion Play of Oberammergau is not ritual, it is drama, like the various films on the life of Christ. One must go further and say that ritual is not primarily a religious activity.

Ritual is part of the language of a culture or society. Corresponding to spoken language, human society uses gestures and signs. Some of these are chosen arbitrarily, like a red traffic light, but once this sign has acquired its significance it conveys its message to everyone in the society. Others, the more important symbols in a culture, acquire their meaning over a long period of time, and seem to have a power of making their point which is much more effective than the mere intention of the one who uses it. The really important points in the life of a people are surrounded by complex clusters of symbols which are called ritual. The clothes worn, the eating habits, the kind of houses lived in are not the arbitrary decisions of our cooks, tailors and builders. Tailors can modify the fashions, but they cannot change what clothing signifies in a society. One's position or role in society, as well as the values which are important to the life of this society, are expressed in the society's rituals. These elaborate sets of customs are usually connected with the pivotal points in human life, like birth, adulthood, marriage and death. Funeral parlours as truly fall under the definition of ritual as do funeral pyres.

Liturgy is the religious ritual of the church, especially the rituals related to the celebration of the sacraments.

The catechism definition of a sacrament was "an outward sign of inward grace." In fact if one replaced the word "grace" by the phrase "what is valued in this society" this definition of a sacrament could be used equally well as a working definition of ritual in general.

We need to be aware, however, that the church also uses nonreligious rituals. Much of the ritual associated with the pope is not strictly liturgical or religious, and certainly not religious in origin. Yet it is often difficult to know where to draw the line, especially among the secondary symbols associated with such a person. Fairy-tales have always made much fun by extravagantly extending the use of words like "royal," down to the "royal stable-boy" and the "royal dust-bin collector"! In the same way one would have to stretch the idea rather far to perceive any valid liturgical meaning in the words: "the papal guards."

Some of the most important work being done at the present day in helping us to understand the Mass and the sacraments comes from a very unlikely source, from anthropologists – scholars associated mostly with the study of primitive tribes. True enough, thirty or forty years ago anthropologists were anything but helpful. They seemed utterly convinced that Christianity was no better than Red Indian Rain Dances or ancient pagan Egyptian or Babylonian myths and ritual.

More recently, however, anthropologists have contributed greatly to our understanding of ritual and symbols. Just at the point when everyone was satisfied that religion and magic were more or less the same, and equally worthless, anthropologists have shown how a people's myths and rituals are of immense importance. Myths and ritual are the ways in which people sum up their whole philosophy of life (their metaphysics); and then, in this whole complex of parables and mimes and dances, pass on their understanding of life from one generation to the next. From our point of view, most interesting of all, is that it has turned out the anthropologists' definitions of ritual are in many

cases very close to the ideas and terminology about the
sacraments that we all learned in the catechism. Quite
unexpectedly, the whole notion of ritual has again become
"respectable" to study, and even to indulge in.

In the years just before the Council, Catholics were
showing embarrassment at much of the criticism of our
elaborate ceremonial. We swallowed hard but were not
quite sure how much truth lay behind remarks like: "ritual
is all mumbo-jumbo, it is superstition, it is only a hangover
from magic." In a flight before that kind of attack, as soon
as the first changes after Vatican II came along, there was
an impulse to abandon anything that might be thought to
have any hint of magic or superstition. For this reason
some wanted to discard vestments, clerical garb, and
religious habits. Many things were disowned at that time,
rituals of all sorts. The rosary was an obvious and very early
casualty. But, even within the Mass, scripture was regarded
by some as being somewhat unsuitable for modern times
and, often enough, it had to give way in favour of readings
from some contemporary writer, Mao's *Little Red Book*, or
anything which could justify itself by being "relevant."
Until the recent reform in the Rite of Reconciliation
(confession), the sacrament of penance too was gradually
being pushed under the carpet. Counselling was acceptable-
lots of respectable people did that – but confession, no. The
new Rite of Reconciliation is just beginning to restore
public confidence in that sacrament among Catholics who
had by and large given it up.

An uncontrolled desire to get rid of useless ceremonial
and decoration had taken hold of some of us, leaving us
with something equivalent to a low-church Protestant or
Calvinist service, where all is clinically reasonable and
logical, with none of "the emotionalism that gets religion
a bad name."

Admittedly there was previously a lot of ceremonial that
could be called questionable. It is good sometimes to
recognise that some of it bordered on the fantastic. You

may remember, for example, the long train worn by the bishop in his full robes in a pontifical procession. It was not a train like that worn by a bride on a wedding gown. It had a great bulge of material in the middle. The acid test of a well trained altar boy was his ability to cope with a bishop's train and not get lost in its billowing folds. The design, you see, dated from the days when bishops always came to the church in procession riding on a horse. The train was made in such a way that, when the bishop got on his horse, the train actually flowed from his shoulders, over the sides and hind-quarters of the horse, down to the ground, carefully obscuring any impropriety the horse might feel like indulging in at an inopportune moment. It was only in 1960 that Pope John did away with that piece of pantomine. Ever so many bits of the pageantry we associated with church ceremonies had really nothing to do with religion. And, in the horror of that discovery, some people wanted to throw out the whole lot.

It is crucial then to be able to decide what is important in ritual and symbol (remembering that in spite of its inappropriateness, the bishop's train was still one of these symbols). How do we judge which of these bits of ritual and ceremonial should be discarded, which should be toned down? How do we know what to emphasise? How do we go about sorting out the symbols in something as complex as a pontifical high Mass, as it was in the days before the Council?

The nearest I have come across to a puzzle of that sort, in an ordinary everyday situation, happened one evening during the Christmas rush, in Woolworths. There were crowds of people milling around everywhere, and as I stood by the counter, a little lady beside me said "hey" peremptorily, "get into the queue." I could not see a queue; but somehow, in the melee, she had constructed a queue, and she knew that it gave her a strict right to be served next. In some way that is what a queue says: it lays claim to be served next. However, if no one else can see the queue, your symbols just cannot do their job, the message does not come through.

This gets us to the central point about symbols: symbols are part of our language, they are part of the way in which we communicate with each other. They are normal, and they are indispensable. But until the anthropologists came to their defence in quite recent years, it was taken for granted by many people that symbols were not really respectable – because they were not logical. It was assumed that if something could not be stated clearly, in words, it was of no use, and should be discarded. Symbols were suspected of being both irrelevant and superfluous.

Strange as it may seem, many people still work on this principle. They think that the Mass has to be readily understandable to any non-Christian who may walk in off the street. (They also usually hold that children cannot cope with symbols unless every bit of it is explained out loud in words.) But the real trouble is their first assumption – that ritual must be able to speak to the non-believer, that its meaning should be clear and obvious to everyone who encounters it, like a stop sign on a road. But any anthropologist will tell you that that is a contradiction in terms. True symbols disclose their meaning only to those who have been initiated. They are part of the language of a culture. It is no fault of the French that people who cannot speak the language cannot understand French poetry, or French humour. Learning the language is the first step in being initiated into a culture. Language, in the wide sense, sets the boundaries of who belongs. The outsider is excluded.

The nature of ritual, or symbols, is that it is a language that conveys its meaning only within a particular community or culture. And learning that language is as slow and as precise an undertaking as, for example, learning French or Samoan well enough to be able to catch all the nuances of meaning in a poem or a conversation or a joke. This, of course, requires more than just knowing the meaning of words. It is inextricably interwoven with the

way these particular people feel about life. Maoritanga or
Fa'a Samoa contain within themselves an understanding
of life which colours everything else, even their jokes.
Only one who has got that inside view can really understand
even the words. Ritual and symbols speak fully only to those
who possess something of this outlook.

In exactly the same way we must recognise clearly that
religious symbols, or the Christian sacraments, really
speak only to those who share the Christian faith. (It is a
lesson to us that someone like Karl Rahner holds strongly
that the Mass should never be televised. You should never
present to people who lack the means for interpreting it
seriously, a series of symbols which inevitably appear
absurd to the outsider. Rahner describes the situation in
which he once sat among a group of non-Christians watch-
ing a televised Mass; they were baffled by it, and their
bafflement soon turned to ridicule.) We might learn from
many primitive peoples, like the Australian Aboriginals,
who still do not allow their ceremonial to be filmed. A
little of an initiation ceremony was once filmed, but only
on condition that the film should never be shown to an
audience containing women!

Symbols therefore, can be understood only within a
particular culture. We shake hands as a greeting; Maoris
press noses (give the hongi); Indians bow, with joined
hands. Within each culture these gestures convey more than
a casual greeting. Each is part of a language that is used
by that particular culture, to express one's relationship
to another. Some of these gestures will be of more importance than others, but together they express, in a way
which words could never do on their own, how these people
understand what life is all about; how these people understand human relationship, and eventually, even how they
perceive the ultimate meaning of life, and of man's relationship to God.

Of course, it is not only religions and primitive people
that use ritual. All this applies whether the group are

Maoris, or Anglo-Saxons or a football club. Every group builds up a whole complex of rituals and patterns of behaviour which do three things:
1. Identify you as a member of the group;
2. Draw a line which clearly excludes the non-member;
3. Sum up the outlook and understanding of life that is shared by those who belong.

Everyone knows what it feels like to walk into a gathering, perhaps in a country pub, or at a meeting in the local hall, and to know immediately that you are a stranger. Sometimes not only are you conscious that you are a stranger, but you know you would never want to be part of that group. Instantly you catch that their values and world view are something you would never want to share. All of this is communicated, almost instantly, through a quite ordinary use of ritual – the way you are greeted, the way certain people do most of the talking, the way people stand or sit.

Let us take a few examples, a lecture, a parish council meeting and a twenty-first birthday party, and do a simple analysis of these three familiar situations.

First, take the example of a lecture. What would someone coming in say about this particular meeting? Obviously it is a working session, it is not a social event or entertainment. One person is standing, lecturing. He is in some position of authority. But it is not a parliament or debate or discussion where everyone has equal standing. At a lecture all listen to one person. There are in fact alternative types of learning situations; the audience could have been broken up into "buzz groups." But anyone coming into a lecture room would recognise that this is a particular kind of relationship or role. It makes a statement about many things we think important.

Again, one could take a meeting of the parish priest and the parish council. Besides getting some of the parish work done, other things are also happening. Perhaps the role of the parish priest is being changed a bit. It is obvious from the parish council meeting that he is no longer seen as the person who makes all the decisions unilaterally. The changes in the relationship between the priest and his people are surfacing in the changes symbolised in the parish council meeting; for example various people take the initiative, someone, other than the parish priest, draws up the agenda, or chairs the meeting.

However, in the next parish, the same sort of meeting might very well be saying that nothing has changed; the parish priest is saying quite clearly "I make all the decisions." In either case, a whole lot of unspoken statements are being made, an alternative to speech, much more powerful than speech. In fact, they are stated in a way that could never be put into words.

A birthday party too can be seen to have many layers of meaning, a twenty-first birthday party, or even the birthday of someone quite young. One may ask when looking at it, "why are all these people here?" Not only the young person's friends and contemporaries are present, but older uncles and aunts who never appear except for weddings and funerals. What is the meaning of the cake, the key, the candles, the speeches? What does all that say about this young person? He is entering into some sort of new relationship within his own particular family group. Therefore the whole group gathers to reassert relationships which could easily be forgotten. Grandparents and other relatives are there, and the young person is made aware of his duties and relationship to them. Even more important, this makes him alert to his responsibility to be enriched by the tradition that they carry. Perhaps also it affirms his responsibility for their care in the future, as they have cared for him in the past. Every bit of that piece of human interchange which is a twenty-first birthday party can be analysed like this to see "what is it saying?" – and it is usually saying things of immense importance.

There is some degree of ritual in all human behaviour, and it is only by a matter of degree that we conclude that a particular thing is primarily ritual or primarily functional. One may open the door for another because his hands are full; one may open the door for him because you are going out together or, one may be "showing him the door," and in that case the action is essentially ritual.

A parish council meeting may be called to arrange a clean up of the grounds. However, that same group of people may, at their next meeting, have exactly the same kind of agenda, but the real business may be principally ritual, symbolic. The parish priest may be re-affirming his role, as to who is in charge. Or the secretary may be staging a bloodless coup, to depose the chairman. In the first example, the work to be done is to the forefront, it is primarily functional. In the other, the role of various people is being asserted or redefined, and we are solidly in the area of ritual.

Ritual is of the essence of all communication between people. The tiny little ritual of putting the salt just out of reach of someone after you have had a tiff lets him know that you have not conceded defeat. In all sorts of little ways we state things that could not be stated in words. Although these examples are rather trivial, ritual usually says things that are quite basic, about our awareness of how we should love, or our awareness of how the world makes sense for us.

Every group or culture or society eventually builds up a whole complex of rituals and symbols that express the core of their understanding of life. Technically this is called the "world view and the ethos" of this particular group. All that life means for a society is encapsulated in its major symbols and rituals.

For the Christian, life makes sense in terms of the death and resurrection of Jesus; our whole world is understood in the light of that great mystery. That is our world view.

A people's ethos means the characteristic manner of behaviour resulting from their world view – the way in which they should relate to one another, the way in which they think they ought to behave. Again, the Christian ethos derives from our world view, and as a result it says – we must treat others with the kind of self-forgetting love Jesus exemplified.

A people's whole philosophy of life, their world view and their ethos, is captured in their major symbols. Especially is this so in their rites for initiating new members, the manner of bringing new members into their group. In these rituals, in particular, their values are passed on to others. The rites of initiation for us Christians are baptism, confirmation and the Eucharist, and the catechumenate by which a new Christian is formed. These three sacraments capture the whole of how life makes sense for a Christian, and how, in consequence, a Christian should respond both to God and to his neighbour.

One of the first things to ask about any group is: what are their dominant symbols? What are the high points in the social life of this particular community? To discover this one might simply ask: what things crop up most in the newspaper? What, for example, are the high points in the social life or the architecture of your own city? If the dominant buildings are all very large, and very ugly and dull pieces of architecture, very inhuman and impersonal, they tell you immediately that people do not matter to those who erected these buildings.

This analysis can be applied to any situation – your own family life, your own community life. What are the important things there? When does your family or community feel that it is one? Perhaps it is just one meal a week, when everyone is present, when those who have moved out from home come back in again. It may be when all are having a snack in the kitchen before going to bed. What are the things seen to be important? In an ordinary family life the dominant factors are things like the working hours of the husband or wife; the very fact that they both have to work. The children's going to school every day makes a very powerful statement about the importance of education in our society. Each of these give strong indicators of what is crucial in our society. No matter what romantic theories we may propound about our priorities, these dominant factors assert emphatically our view of life and the world.

In any such exercise as this we are trying to discover the dominant symbols. On these our whole system of values, our understanding of life, hinges: education, labour, Sundays with the family, and relaxation together, the health of the community and of the family, the amount of money paid, for example on insurance policies. How much overtime work has to be taken on in order to afford education and health insurance? Or is overtime paying for a second car, a boat and a house by the sea? Dominant symbols begin to sort themselves out; they fall into a rank. Work may be providing just the necessities for supporting a family, or it may be concerned with status symbols to confirm your sense of security.

When we come to religion, and in particular to Christianity, the dominant symbols are already catalogued for us. The seven dominant symbols are, of course, the seven sacraments; the seven crucial events in which the Christian community expresses in its totality, its own understanding of the world, and of how life does make sense. These seven symbols mark off the key points in life: birth, marriage, death, adulthood, sickness, leadership. The daily Eucharist adds another dimension to the wonder of daily life itself. Together, these seven events express the whole of the Christian's world view, and the whole of the Christian's ethos, his sense of being called to be a child of the Father, and called to love, as we are being loved by the Father.

Yet, even within these seven symbols of Christianity, there is also a hierarchy of importance. All are clustered around the Mass. The Mass affirms that it is not the critical points of birth, marriage, death, that are the highest importance, but life itself.

In the early 1800's, just before Catholic emancipation in 1828, an English historian, puzzling over the failure to get rid of Catholicism in Ireland, gave as his conclusion the now famous phrase "It is the Mass that matters." Because of their failure to obliterate the Mass, the faith survived.

Yet, I wonder, has that very phrase "it is the Mass that matters" thrown all other six dominant symbols into semi-obscurity. Have we got into the situation where no sacrament seems to be thought worth celebrating unless it is tucked into the folds of the Eucharistic liturgy.

In the early Church, baptism was the great, crucial and formative sacrament; it has been called the earliest "popular devotion." Huge chunks of the New Testament were actually baptismal formulae. The first Epistle of St. Peter, for example, is made up of a pre-baptismal sermon in Chapter 2, and a post-baptismal sermon in Chapter 3. Many of the hymns in the Letters of St. Paul were baptismal hymns, used in the early liturgy.

Perhaps part of the impoverishment of symbols which we are witnessing is due to the fact that the other sacraments are not being taken to be, in the true sense, a way in which Christ is really present. We have narrowed the idea of the Real Presence, so that we regard it as applying only to transubstantiation. Unwittingly then this was symbolised in the last few centuries by having just minimal rituals, or very hastily performed rituals, for baptism or weddings and the other sacraments. Until recently, if there was not a nuptial Mass, a wedding took seven minutes.

Even today, after all the reforms, we are tending again to downgrade the other sacraments, by always inserting them into the Mass, as though they were inadequate on their own, as though they were not a Real Presence. The introduction to the new rite for baptism does not support the now-common practice of having baptism at the last Mass on Sunday, on the first Sunday of each month. Baptism must not constantly obtrude into the regular Sunday cycle. But, more important, infant baptism is normally to be celebrated as a sacrament in its own right, outside of the Mass.

A symbol never comes to us on its own. It is always set in a cluster of other symbols, the secondary symbols. The dominant symbol may be a meeting of the parish council, but all sorts of things can modify and change what is going to happen there. Perhaps, usually the meeting is held in the presbytery, with everyone relaxed in the sitting room; but this month the meeting is moved to the school classroom, with the parish priest sitting up front and everyone else in the desks. There is no need to tell people that the atmosphere is different, that something else is going on. Or maybe, the parish chairman invites people to meet at his house, so that now he is the host, and the parish priest is the guest.

Theology, and for the most of us that means the catechism (or its modern equivalent), gives the impression that it is all quite easy to see that the Mass is about a meal of real bread and wine, over which the Eucharistic institution words have been recited; that this dominant symbol is obvious immediately. But that is the least obvious fact about the Mass as we commonly experience it. Over the centuries the dominant symbol – one cup of wine, one loaf of bread, blessed and broken – has been dehydrated; and then in later centuries it became smothered in a mountain of secondary symbols. In the days of the Latin Mass, you will remember we never saw those symbols, the bread and wine, except for a moment when the bread was held above the priest's head. If you were at the back of the church you never saw it at all.

Part of our task in the renewal of the liturgy is to achieve a balance again between the statements that are being made by the dominant symbol and those being made by the other rites which accompany it.

Let us take a few examples. Firstly, some indicating the impoverishment of the dominant symbols as we regularly experience them.

In the liturgy of the Word, because of the position of the priest's chair in many churches, he disappears from sight or loses contact with the congregation when he sits down for the readings. Similarly, if the scripture lesson is read from the back page of the Catholic newspaper, the symbolic importance of the bible (or lectionary) as the Church's sacred book, is destroyed. Christianity too is a religion of the Book. It is worthwhile some time to go to a service at the Jewish Synagogue and watch the awe and reverence with which the sacred scrolls of the Scriptures are taken from the tabernacle (or as it is still called – the Holy of Holies). It is with exactly the same reverence, or even more, that the Church views the Old and New Testaments: the Word of the Word made flesh.

In the liturgy of the Eucharist the impoverishment of the dominant symbols is seen in three glaringly obvious instances of failure to conform to the Church's official decrees.

1. It is two centuries since the instruction was first issued by Benedict XIV that communion ought to be given from hosts consecrated at that Mass. The instruction has been repeated in every decree of recent years, but still the tabernacle is used as a supply larder. The rubric faces the priest every day on the page of the missal containing the prayers for the preparation of the gifts. The tabernacle is principally for the needs of the sick. There should be absolutely no trafficking between the altar and the tabernacle during the Mass.

2. Similarly, the decrees of recent years lay down that the bread should "look like bread, have the appearance of bread, taste like bread, and be able to be broken like bread," so that it can express obviously the meaning of St. Paul's description of the Eucharist: "we are one body, because we have eaten of the one loaf." It must taste like bread; it must certainly not be so flimsy that it melts in the mouth before it can be swallowed. On that point St Thomas is quite clear that this sacrament consists of the eating and drinking. One must not think of oneself as a tabernacle in which the host, the presence of Christ, rests in one's mouth or stomach for fifteen minutes, until it is digested. The

essential symbol is that of being nourished with food. For this reason, St. Thomas himself is said to have always taken a full chalice of wine at Mass. It is drinking, in order to be nourished. The experience of being nourished is the sacramental sign.

3. That, of course, leads immediately to the third example – why cannot we have communion under both kinds normally? The Lord's command is unquestionably clear – "take and drink this all of you, this is my Blood." The rule in many dioceses is simply that communion may be given under both species at any time when it is convenient and can be done with dignity.

As a last example, that word "dignity" calls to mind the rush with which communion is so often distributed. Communion-time is the most precious moment in the life of the individual, and nothing so trivial as getting the cars out of the carpark should force it to become hasty and irreverent. As St. Exupery said in the *Little Prince* "it is the time you have wasted on your rose that makes your rose precious to you." We need to be more ready to waste time on God.

Each of these examples are simple things. They show how major change can be achieved without having to bully the congregation. But it does demand of us that we concentrate our efforts on implementing the core elements, the dominant symbols in our liturgy. No matter how slowly we move, let us ensure that we are going in the right direction, and that we give primary importance to the things that are primary, that is, the Word and the sacred meal of bread and wine. Sometimes congregations resist getting involved in the liturgy because of their accurate instinct for seeing that what we want to involve them in is only peripheral.

A further technique to analyse what is happening at any particular piece of liturgy is simply to ask: who says what? (who talks, and who does not talk?).

Take an example. Once or twice it has happened to me when saying Mass in a parish church on a Sunday, that when I sat down for the readings, the ten year old altar-boy got up and went to the lectern, and read all the readings, up to the Gospel. Now the first question this raises is: who should do the readings? The decrees are emphatic that each person should perform the parts appropriate to his particular role, and no others. The acolyte should not also be the reader. Further, the readers of the first reading, of the psalm, and of the second reading, the leader of the prayers of the faithful, should be different people. This reflects the variety of gifts or charisms which the Spirit gives to the Church to build it into the Body of Christ.

One may go on to ask: what else does it say if a ten year old does the readings at a Sunday parish Mass? Can a ten year old be the liturgical leader to adult Christians? Of course, it is quite normal for a child to read at a Mass for children, even if adults are present in small numbers. But just from the point of view of the dynamics of any adult gathering, a child cannot be the chairman, a child cannot be the principal speaker. Seen from this point of view, as liturgical leaders, this raises an enormous question mark about altar-boys; and it shows also that the whole debate about altar-girls is completely off beam. That is not where the real problem lies. The question is not whether we should have altar-girls, but whether in a Mass for adults we should have altar-children.

A further aspect of the question: "who says what?" surfaces when this is applied to the congregation. Which parts do the people feel at ease in "joining in?" The people usually say or sing the Sanctus, the Acclamation and Agnus Dei quite readily; but no amount of pressure, of father walking up and down the aisle beefing out the hymn, can get a squeak out of congregations at other parts of the Mass. It is worth noticing how a congregation resists every effort to get them to join in lustily in parts which they sense are really not important.

As a final summation of the most important aspects of this chapter, I would conclude:-

1.   The high-point of the Christian's prayer and profession of faith in the Death and Resurrection is the utterly silent eating of the Bread and Wine. "When we eat this bread and drink this cup . . . ." It is in this that we proclaim that life makes sense for us in terms of Christ's death and resurrection. This is the supreme example of the phrase: "symbols not only do things, they say things."

2.   Not only that, but these symbols are the main way in which God reveals himself to us. (That is what we mean when we say they are sacraments.) Looking at the Bread and Wine, and in eating it, the Lord reveals his presence to us and within us.

4 PREPARATION OF THE ALTAR AND THE GIFTS.

IMPLICITLY, in talking about silence and the cluttered vestibule, we touched on two of the most important conditions needed if the liturgy of the Word is to emerge as something of value in its own right. What is first required is merely that it be given a chance. In fact, unless one has experienced the liturgy of the Word as a sacrament of major importance in its own right, one is in no position to evaluate it or to criticise it. Chapter 8 will return to a more detailed discussion of this part of the Mass.

Moving now into the liturgy of the Eucharist, it is important to apply the ideas discussed in the last chapter on ritual, so as to discover some of the things that are going wrong in that part of the Mass. The problems can be divided into two areas:

1. Those caused by our tendency to overstress bits of ritual and symbolism which are really secondary.

2. Those caused by a defective theology of the Eucharist, which leads on to distort the symbols, making them say what one wrongly presumes they are supposed to be saying. Mistaken theory, leads to distortion of the symbols.

Stressing secondary parts of ritual is most often caused by the fact that the important parts of the ritual have been handled with such excessive reverence that they have been almost moved off stage. There is nothing left for the congregation but the peripheral, since the priest monopolizes the essentials.

The other side of this coin however, is the assumption that only what the priest does is essential, and therefore, it matters little what the congregation are put to do: singing hymns, saying the rosary, or forming offertory processions, make your choice.

The liturgy of the Word and liturgy of the Eucharist do seem to be so clerically dominated that the people get frustrated. Consequently, no-one should be surprised that the congregation want to take over bits of the priest's parts, for example, joining in saying the Eucharistic Prayer or joining in the final doxology "Through Him, With Him, In Him." To show that there is not a basic discrimination against the laity, it ought to be sufficient reply that even in a concelebrated Mass, only the principal celebrant says the Eucharistic Prayer aloud, the other celebrants should recite it inaudibly. Too many priests, however, forget that the directives say that "each person should do those parts, and those parts only, which belong to that particular role." They work on the principle that if it is important, the priest should say it, and he should say it aloud; and if the priest does not say it, it is not important. Traditionally, the two parts which belong essentially to the role of the presiding priest are the homily and the Eucharistic Prayer.

Therefore, all other parts should be done by a whole range of other ministers: readers, leaders of the psalm and of prayers of the faithful, choir, commentators. If the celebrant however, has gobbled up everyone else's role, it is not surprising that the congregation feels it must make the most of the bits that are left – the entrance rite, and the preparation of the gifts. It is not surprising that these very unimportant secondary elements are given so much emphasis and attention in congregational participation.

Before moving to the second point, another flaw should be noted. There is a general assumption that participation is judged by the quantity of words any particular person says. This assumption is also, of course, linked to the idea of the Mass as so much text to be read through. Since the priest seems to have a disproportionate amount to say, the inclination to even off the score asserts itself by giving the congregation long hymns to sing, or things to recite.

What is totally neglected is the fact that we participate most of all by our gestures. Remember, for example, the liturgy of Good Friday. The two dominant symbols in that long liturgy are the Cross and the Prostration, going down, if possible full length on the floor, lying there until one has some sense of being, as it were, dust before his feet. The prostration is used four times in the Good Friday liturgy, but the degree of involvement that that evokes, totally outweighs the hour and a half of words which surround it, and give it its meaning.

We must pay more attention to our bodily involvement – beating our breast, kneeling, joining our hands, bowing, looking, using our hands and arms, standing, sitting at ease, learning to walk as an act of religion, walking to the altar of God. Only when the value of gesture has been re-affirmed, will people get rid of the bugbear of not having enough to say. They will cease to feel competitive about the priest or the official ministers.

The second source of ritual distortion is a defective theory about what is going on; in this case a defective theology of the Eucharist produces unbalanced liturgy. This manifests itself most especially in regard to what used to be called the Offertory Rite. The name for this part of the Mass was changed. Its correct name is the Preparation of the Gifts. Note that the term is not the "presentation of gifts" as one sometimes sees it called. In the new rite the offertory prayer is the prayer which the priest says immediately after the consecration: "In memory of his death and resurrection we offer you Father . . . ."

The fact that most people still talk about the offertory and about offertory processions should make us aware that they still think of this part of the Mass as our offering of our gifts and our lives to the Lord; later on, the priest will offer Christ's sacrifice to God. Many priests say such things as "here you make your sacrifice." But there is only one offering, not two offerings. The one offering takes place in the Eucharistic Prayer, in which the congregation and the priest are drawn into the single offering which Christ made of himself to the Father.

A look back into history shows that we are not dealing with a minor and recent misinterpretation, but something that has been developing since the 14th century.

Anyone who remembers the Mass in the old Dominican Rite will recall that the priest put the wine and water into the chalice before Mass began. Then when he came to the so-called "offertory" he simply said one verse of Psalm 115 (Quid retribuam Domino . . .); he washed his hands, and said the secret prayer (Super secreta – the prayers over the things set aside), and then continued straight into the Preface.

The Dominican Rite was in fact simply the Roman Rite in the 13th century. Around 1260 the fifth Master-General laid down a uniform rite for the celebration of Mass throughout the Order. For this, he chose the rite used in the Papal curia at the time. This uniform rite then remained unchanged in the Order over the next couple of centuries. All the other prayers that used to be said in the Roman Rite until 1965 were accretions over the three centuries from 1250 to 1550. Until 1550, every diocese was free to make its own local adaptations and minor changes, until Pius V stabilised the Roman Rite in 1567. At that time the Pope allowed any rite to continue if it had been in use unchanged for 200 years. The Roman Rite (or Tridentine Mass, as we have now come to call it), was simply the Franciscan Rite in the 1550's. Because of the popularity of the Franciscans, and the fact that so many priests were Franciscan Tertiaries, it was the most widespread rite in the West. Pius V, therefore, made it the uniform rite. The so-called "Dominican Rite" was not really a distinct rite, it was a form of the Roman Rite, which had been preserved unchanged since 1250.

The story becomes more curious as we discover how all those extra prayers in the old offertory had originated. It was all very strange, and quite untheological. As music and polyphony developed in those centuries, longer and longer musical settings were composed for the offertory antiphon and psalm. What had once been a brief line of plainchant grew to a lengthy musical performance, during which the priest twiddled his thumbs, waiting until it was over. Then gradually, priests started flipping through the missal, reading various prayers from here and there. Over the centuries a fairly uniform group of prayers came to be used. You will find the origin of each of them in Jung-mann's book, *The Mass in the Roman Rite*. One or two of these prayers were prefaces, one of the others came from an ancient Eucharistic prayer, some were post-communion prayers.

So, at the end of three centuries, the priest had got to the stage where he was quietly saying to himself what was almost equivalent to a whole Eucharistic liturgy, while the choir sang their prolonged setting of the offertory verse.

In the later development of polyphonic Masses, the Sanctus was usually so long that the priest used to carry on saying the Eucharistic Prayer in silence. Just before the consecration, he waited until the choir finished the first half of the Sanctus. Then, after the words of Institution and the elevation, the choir continued the Sanctus: "Blessed is He who comes . . . ." In the meanwhile, the priest finished the Eucharistic Prayer, and again had to wait before singing the Great Doxology: "Per ipsum et cum ipso et in ipso . . . ."

In 1567 therefore, Pius V made the Franciscan Rite uniform for the whole Latin Church, and this collection of private meditations of the priest was given a permanent place in the liturgy.

The historical origins of the offertory prayers were, in time, forgotten. Then, particularly in the 17th and 18th centuries, there developed a whole series of theories to explain the supposed theological meaning of these prayers. It really was a theological conundrum to explain this offering before the offering. Many suggestions were made, the most common being that the people make their offering of themselves first, and then, later on, the priest offers Christ's sacrifice to the Father.

Added to this, in the 18th century it became popular to follow Mass by associating each part of the Mass with a detail of Our Lord's passion. For example, as the priest washed his hands, we thought of Pilate washing his hands. You see what was happening. Instead of seeing the Mass as a sacrament or symbol, or ritual, it was coming to be interpreted as a mime – a sort of passion play.

The explanations of the Mass which most of us received in our catechism in school, were in fact, directly connected with these theological theories of the 17th to 19th centuries. Some of these theories practically gained such a monopoly that they are still assumed to be the basic unquestionable explanation of the faith. Probably the most common is the theory that the Mass is a sacrifice because the two separate consecrations symbolise the separation of the Body and Blood of Christ, and therefore, his death. Somehow Christ's death is mimed, and therefore, it is made to happen all over again.

It was only in the 1920's that St. Thomas' basic teaching on symbolism and sacraments re-emerged. One of the very important books at the time was Abbot Vonier's *Key to the Doctrine of the Eucharist*, still a fine book, which beautifully explains St. Thomas' meaning. That book was one of the theological factors that made the liturgical reform possible, because it rediscovered the older theological tradition on the meaning of the word "sacrament." Good theology once more made good liturgy possible. Good theology does not guarantee good liturgy, but you cannot make good liturgy out of bad theology.

The rite of the old offertory has changed into the simple ceremony of preparing the bread and wine and the altar, yet many people seem to think that this was done just to shorten the ceremony, the significance of which remained the same. Many presume that it still is about the congregation's offering of themselves. They, therefore, try to put back in expanded ritual what has been eliminated from the text. As a result, offertory procesions have become one of the most pronounced expressions of congregational participation. An incorrect piece of theology is now being enacted more emphatically than ever before. Until 1967, all those prayers at the offertory were recited silently by the priest, and even his actions were not visible, since he had his back to the people. The offertory is now no longer there. The preparation of the gifts is that, and nothing more.

Fr. Clifford Howell in an article in *Clergy Review* (Feb. 1977) says:

"The General Instruction on the Roman Missal, 12, explains that the very nature of the presidential prayers requires that they be spoken audibly and clearly, and everyone should listen to them with attention." GIRM 13, referring to the other type of prayer "said by the priest in his personal capacity" adds that "Prayers of this kind are said inaudibly" (The Latin is "secreto"). Hence the distinction is clear to the people: audible prayers are presidential and the people should "listen with attention." Inaudible prayers are personal and private; the people need not attend to them, but remain free to say their own prayers if they want.

"Such are the prayers at the Preparation of the Gifts – the whole lot of them up till 'Pray brethren' – and the four private prayers between the Our Father and the Communion. The rubric bids the priest to say them 'secreto.' Unfortunately somebody (not ICEL) translated 'secreto' as 'quietly.' This is not satisfactory because ambiguous. It is possible to speak quietly, yet audibly. And that is what quite a lot of priests are doing. Why? Perhaps because they are misled by the mistranslation 'quietly.' But more probably because they think 'these prayers are so beautiful.'

"Indeed they are beautiful, but that does not authorise the priest to obscure the distinction between presidential and private prayer, and to deny to the people the 'sacred silence' which is their due. 'Meaningful silence is an element in celebration which must be given its due place.'

"One must concede that the rubric 'secreto' is qualified by another rubric covering just the prayers said by the priest as he holds up the paten and then the chalice 'aliquantulum' (therefore not high up). If there is no music going on it is then lawful to say those prayers (but only those two prayers) out loud, and for the people to answer 'Blessed be God for ever.' But it is not compulsory to do that. The people may be left in silence. Priests who use the 'permissive rubric' for the two named prayers, though they intrude slightly on the 'sacred silence,' do not destroy it completely; nor do they completely destroy the sign showing that the 'preparation prayers' are not presidential (for they are not said 'extensis manibus'). The distinction, however, is somewhat weakened by the audibility. Thus emphasis on 'secreto' is not mere rubricism; it is motivated by a desire to preserve a distinguishing sign which not only helps the people to understand the difference in importance between presidential and private prayers, but also gives them a respite which will help them to concentrate more fruitfully.

"Why do the wrong thing when it is just as easy to do the right thing – or something very like the right thing?"

In a footnote he adds:

"The 'inside story' of the Preparation of the Gifts is interesting. The reforming body, the Consilium, contained members appointed because of their expertise in liturgy, but also others appointed just because they were officials of certain Roman congregations. The liturgists wanted priest and people to be left free during the whole rite of Preparation until the presidential Prayer over the Gifts. No specified texts till then, [i.e. more or less like the old Dominican Rite]. But the curial party wanted specified texts spoken out loud – i.e. still more words! After much argument the compromise was reached; prescribed texts, but 'secreto.' But finally, shortly before publication of the revised Ordo Missae, the curialists managed to pull certain strings and got the 'permissive rubric' inserted into the definitive edition."

In a later article, (*Clergy Review*, July 1977), reviewing the new missal published by the German hierarchy in 1976, Clifford Howell adds the following comment:

"In the German missal all items which, according to the rubrics, are to be said *secreto* are printed in slightly smaller type. In our missal the word *secreto* has been mistranslated as 'quietly,' whereas it ought to be 'inaudibly.' The word 'quietly' is ambiguous. As a result some priests here say the private prayers of the Preparation of the Gifts and those preceding the Communion in a voice which is audible (even though quiet). German priests are not misled into such an error; in fact they are even led in the opposite direction. *Per se* all the offertory prayers fall under the rubric *secreto*, but there is a qualification for two of them: the prayers accompanying the lifting up of the bread, and then of the wine, may be said audibly 'if no offertory song is sung.' The German Missal of course notes this exception, but adds a comment: 'since the people have been listeners throughout the Liturgy of the Word, and must again listen to the audible Eucharistic Prayer, the priest may do well not to miss the opportunity for giving them a sacred silence; he may refrain from using the permission to say these two prayers out loud.'"

Therefore, firstly, we must notice that most of the offertory hymns or "gift-songs" in our hymnals are theologically wrong. Mostly they are popular metrical versions of the old offertory prayers. These hymns, if they belong anywhere, could perhaps belong after the Great Amen, before the Our Father. The missal says that the *Amen* may be expanded – although, if it is to be expanded, it would probably be preferable to do so by repeating the Eucharistic Acclamation.

Secondly, and even more importantly, this part of the Mass, the preparation of the gifts, is just a time to relax one's concentration. A little quiet is needed, not necessarily a rigid silence; perhaps some quiet organ music, to help prepare for the next point of high involvement.

As for the collection – well there is no harm in doing the housekeeping here. The General Instruction, para. 49, says that this is also a time to collect gifts or money for the poor. These are to be laid in a suitable place, but not on the altar. Therefore, it implies that the collection should not be brought to the priest.

There is strong reason to think that the collection really belongs to the end of the liturgy of the Word, rather than the beginning of the liturgy of the Eucharist. In the early church the deacon had the office of caring for the needy and the poor of the parish. For this reason especially, the deacon was the leader of the prayers of the faithful; he knew what the needs were, he knew best what to pray for. Thirdly, in turn, it was the deacon who distributed to the needy all that the community had given in the collection. It is much more likely then, that the collection was related to the process of first praying for the needy, and then making some contribution for them. For obvious reasons too, the collection was probably taken up before the catechumens were sent home, that is, before the preparation of gifts and the beginning of the liturgy of the Eucharist.

Of course, there are times when fittingly, the preparation of gifts can be done more elaborately. In Samoan custom, for instance, on special occasions, a fine mat is brought to lay on the altar.

We must also bear in mind that what is said here about a rather low-key preparation of the gifts is not just a question of personal whim. There is underlying it too, a very important principle in prayer. In prayer we need to be not always under pressure, with the consequent tendency to recite the prayers non-stop, relentlessly, as sometimes happens when people are saying the Psalm or the Creed or the Our Father. As in saying the rosary in years gone by, or in reciting the Latin Office, pressure causes prayers to become a relentless tumble of words. Prayer needs a sense of a lack of busyness. Like love, prayer is quite useless. It is not done for ulterior motives. In the best sense it is a sheer waste of time. We must have a glad, easy delight in wasting time, admiring God. A sense that everything must be productive, and go like clockwork, is utterly destructive of prayer. Prayer needs times of decompression beween the periods of deep involvement. The preparation of the gifts admirably serves this purpose, between the readings and the Eucharistic Prayer. But to achieve this it needs to be relaxed. There must not be a new demand for attention on the pretext that "this is where we make our offering of our own lives, and this is therefore the highpoint of our participation."

The following two points on this part of the Mass are basic:

(i)   This section of the Mass should be a period of repose. Instrumental music is to be preferred, or the choir may sing an anthem.

(ii) If there is song at this time of the Mass, the theme of of the text should "reflect" the theme of the Readings or the Season of the Church's Year. (Eucharistic songs tend to anticipate the Eucharistic Prayer.)

5 NOISE AS RITUAL

THE TITLE of Ralph Keifer's article *The Noise of our Solemn Assemblies* (Worship, Jan. 1971) displays a very happy choice of words. Obviously the phrase "Solemn Assemblies" immediately alerts us to the fact that we are talking about very special kinds of gathering. This is not the noise of people on a railway platform waiting for a train; clearly we are in the formal situation of ritual.

The word "noise" also enables us to see that it is not enough to speak about "Music in the Liturgy." One first has to deal with the significance of the whole range of audible sounds, from speech to song, to church bells ringing. "Noise" as used here is not necessarily an ugly word, nor is it meant to be disparaging. Perhaps he could have used the word "sounds," but that is rather weak. "The Noise of our Solemn Assemblies" excludes background noises like the rumble of coughing through the sermon, shuffling of feet, or the occasional clatter of a kneeler or a baby crying; but it includes all those noises deliberately done in such a gathering, in fact it covers the whole topic of *noise as ritual*, or noise as sacrament.

Previously, we dealt with silence and stillness as a preparation for Mass. Now we must look at the use of silence and sounds as themselves parts of ritual – sounds of all sorts; bells, speaking, singing, organ music, the clapping of hands.

Just take the example of clapping, although it is probably not the best example to start on because clapping is usually a response to someone else's action, rather than being a starter in the ritual process. But, what an extraordinary thing to do! Furthermore, there are so many ways of doing it. There is the single peremptory clap to reprimand someone; the slow clap to express your disapproval of the batsman's stone walling, and the glamorous clap of applause in approval of what someone has said. Clapping is a way in our culture that a crowd registers its assent, like cheering. Cheering does not use any particular words, it just makes a great noise of approval. This is what the psalms so often refer to:

Ps. 149 – Shout for joy to the Lord all the earth.

Ps. 66 – Make a joyful noise for the Lord.

Ps. 99 – Cry out with joy . . . acclaim the Lord.

We might say that singing is a refined way of shouting or cheering. It is refined in the sense of being more subtle, therefore also able to adapt itself to different occasions and to express various shades of meaning and of involvement. Clapping, as has been said, is more of a response to something already done.

The first distinguishing feature we notice in our analysis of noise as ritual, is the way in which sounds are used as signals to a group of people, making them alert to the fact that they are entering into the area of ritual, into the area of religion and the sacred.

The question to be asked then is: What is the best kind of signal for this entering into ritual, sacred place and time? Anglican liturgy speaks of it as "The Call to Worship." What form of call should we use? What is the best way to call people to attention? It is more than a call to attention; people are being invited to make the passage into the area of the sacred, of ritual.

It seems to be taken for granted that this is done by singing a hymn. An entrance hymn is the unquestioned technique for gathering a congregation together as one.

But, striking a bell or gong can be equally effective, as in the Abbey Theatre; there is not stage curtain, but after the gong strikes, in ten seconds the attention is rivetted. The same is true of temple bells, church bells, or altar bells.

But we also should not forget that at a Quaker meeting everyone sits in silence until, as they say: "the meeting is gathered," until a sense of unity has taken hold of the group. The signal is that silence – a certain quality in the silence. At this point we might learn from the Quakers that silence needs to be silent – dare I say without "soft music," the airline music piped through the aircraft to calm nervous passengers with a sort of aural massage. We have to learn to cope with silence – to venture into the emptiness, where God is met.

Implicitly, you will notice that all these are much more than a mere call to attention. Each is a very simple rite of transition from the casual everyday world, into the world of mystery and God. One needs to observe, on the other hand, usually all that may be achieved by an "opening hymn" at Mass is that it drowns the clatter of the late-comers getting into their seats.

It seems to me that the main reason why the opening hymn fails to do anything, is that such formal singing cannot really work unless the crowd are already somewhat united, or at least a sufficient proportion of the crowd is united, so that they can gradually gather up the others as their singing proceeds. Nothing is really more likely to make people feel not a part of things as a hymn sung by a few straggling voices here and there, following one strong voice of the priest or choir master gallantly beefing out the verses. It seems that other *signals of the sacred* are needed before a congregation can be sufficiently "gathered" (in the Quaker sense) to be able to sing a hymn, to feel comfortable about singing together. It is not just that the people do not know the words or the tune or that they cannot sing. What has gone wrong is that we have not paid attention to the dynamics of ritual. There has to be a transition from ordinary behaviour to ritual behaviour. There have to be certain signals of the sacred to make the transition from the chatting which nowadays will go on even in the church – the little informal whispered gossips – to the entry into this new sphere.

This ritual process occurs even at a football match. There is the ritual of the crowd gathering and chatting, and then the very pronounced ritual of the two teams running in formal lines onto the field; there is no other word for it but ritual. It captures the attention, builds up expectations, before the main ritual begins, with a celebrity to throw in the ball. Football matches are ritual too. At a cinema, it is the drawing of the curtain (even though we do not need a curtain, since there is no stage to cover); even a cinema needs a ritual for gathering the audience by some signal, to make them aware that we are now moving into the world of fantasy.

There is a further important factor to be noted. Not infrequently, the type of response that we ask for is not appropriate for this particular group, or at this particular time. Perhaps at the end of the Mass they might be able to sing lustily, but that particular music or hymn will not do for an opening. Usually we have to work up to the atmosphere of unselfconscious involvement. Wholehearted involvement cannot be evoked instantly. Everything needs a warming up period: singers sing scales, athletes do physical jerks. But people seem to expect instant wholehearted involvement from a church congregation. It is noticeable that even charismatic meetings, which we take for granted to be the epitome of unselfconscious spontaneity, in fact build up quite slowly. Charismatic groups, of course, are lucky that they are not crippled by the sense of having to be finished in forty-five minutes, or to reach a religious climax within the first ten to fifteen minutes.

One must recognise that, no matter how long the service is to last, one has to observe how the dynamics of ritual work. If one is planning for a religious service of thirty minutes, or fifty minues, one has to work on quite a different scale than would be used in a concert which lasts two hours, or a football match, for that matter. Do you remember that disastrous anticlimax a few years ago, when Mohammed Ali knocked out his opponent, Sonny Liston, in the first round? It was all over in one and a half minutes of the match. No one had had a chance to get involved, before it was all over. I am sure that is how the Philistines must have felt that day when David threw stones at Goliath. Involvement cannot happen instantly, at the flick of a switch.

Music and singing can, of course, act as excellent signals to call us into the presence of God. Frequently it is, however, demanding too much from a congregation, who are not much accustomed to singing together, to come in cold and then expect them instantly to sing heartily.

Before looking for practical guidelines on the type of singing best suited to a particular group, a distinction made by sociologists must be borne in mind; a triple distinction between a small group, a crowd, and a throng:

- a small group of a maximum size of about twenty; a group which is small enough for each of those in it to know each other moderately well;
- a crowd, such as we have at a Sunday Mass; or a secondary group. It should be noted that for an effective "crowd" it needs to be a network of "small groups."
- a throng, an enormous crowd such as one gets at a rally.

Quite different dynamics are required to operate each of these three.

Even the small group needs to be subdivided again into a formal group and an informal group.

A formal group has some kind of permanent structure, such as a group that lives together, or that meets or works together, spending a lot of its time together. A religious community is a small group, with a formal structure and permanence. In such a group there are accepted signals, which can tune people in on a particular activity quite quickly. In an ordinary office the clatter of tea cups signals morning tea break in the office. The bell ringing for prayer works in the same way in a religious house. Jean Vanier gave the example of their community at Trosly where every evening, at the end of the evening meal, two candles were lit on the table. Over the years this gesture has acquired the power to evoke an immediate response; chatter, or the tensions of the day, are forgotten and all enter a calm time of praying together. Gregorian chant is another highly developed and subtle signal, to one who is attuned to it, which leads to the dispositions needed for contemplative prayer. A formal group acquires highly developed responsiveness to a particular signal, even if it is only the rattle of tea-cups.

On the other hand, the informal group, like the group of young people sitting around in a flat, works on quite different dynamics. Such a small group will, for example, use music quite differently. Most likely just one person sings solo, with a guitar. The others will sit, listening, or at best, will sing sotto voce. The formality of disciplined singing, as by a choir, or of a type of music which requires a well-disciplined vocal production, like a Bach hymn, is quite unsuitable for this kind of group. The same would probably apply to a house Mass. In this regard, one often hears of house Masses where no adaptation is made. Extravagant innovation is not needed, but a house Mass is not meant to be a Sunday parish Mass, said in somebody's lounge. A small group Mass requires quite different dynamics, and quite different music.

One great trap for the unwary in the Decree on Music in the Liturgy, May 1967, is that it speaks of three degrees of active participation, and then immediately assigns certain things to be sung according to each "degree of participation." Almost unnoticed it has slipped in the equation "participation" equals "singing."

Apart from participation by listening and looking, there is the vocal assent which may express itself in anything from a low grunted *Amen* to a great cheer. Do not too readily despise the gentle grunt: "em, good"! The gentle grunt may not rank as very sublime poetry, or as music, yet it is a way in which, in our society, we give our consent to quite important decisions in our lives, quite sincerely. I feel quite sure most people assented to the proposal to marriage with no more than a half-spoken "Yeah." So do not blame people too much if they cannot readily sing in four parts, like Welshmen at a rugby match. Do not blame them too much if they do not articulate clearly; it does not prove that they are uninvolved.

This does not excuse us from learning a more adequate and appropriate way than grunting for saying "thanks" and expressing our love, and our admiration of God. But not everyone can write poems to the one he loves, although everyone does try to find words to express his love.

Music in ritual can then be approached in a number of ways. First of all, music as a *signal*, calling the group to attention, to be aware of why they are gathered, alerting them to some degree of their identity as a particular group, rather than a mere collection of pepole. Take the example of a crowd of people having meals in a restaurant, a number of small groups, unrelated, except by physical proximity. Then a band starts playing, or a singer comes on, and suddenly they all switch over, to become at least superficially, a *crowd*, with a common point of human contact (human as distinguished from mere "physical proximity").

Secondly, music can also be part of the very experiencing of being at one with all those other people if, for example, they agree to listen. How often one notices in a restaurant when a band begins to play, nobody pays any attention. They do not agree to listen, but just talk on. In that case they are not giving their consent to being summoned to be one *group*. The music remains only background noise, but not a focus of attention.

Thirdly, the experience of oneness is enhanced even more if all sing together, as in a German beer garden.

Fourthly, in the area of religion one has to go further and say that there is a way in which music is part of the very experiencing of God's presence, which occurs in liturgy; it is not merely decoration. One does not have to sing; one may just listen to others sing. Once more, notice that consenting to listen, or consenting to join in, is equivalent to agreeing to submit to this liturgical rite; you allow yourself to be pulled into something, drawn into something, much more powerful than yourself. Music is so much a part of the total ritual activity that it can be, not only a call to worship, like an army bugle call to get up, but more importantly, it can be part of the sacrament itself, in which we experience God's presence. A piece of music (like the singing of a National anthem, or the the the singing of Credo III at an international gathering of pilgrims at Lourdes or Rome), immediately enables you to identify yourself with that group – as on St. Patrick's day at the Irish Club, when we all sing "Hail Glorious St. Patrick." It does not matter that the tune is bad, and the words are terrible; somehow it does epitomise for us (Irish) our sense of belonging to this long heritage of Catholicism, bequeathed to us by so many centuries of saints. St. Patrick's Breastplate, and the spirituality that is summed up there, is caught in the first line of that pathetic music.

The American bishops issued a directive on music in the liturgy, which is quite astounding as we look back on it and see all the things we did not do, which were so accurately and well-described there.

"We are Christians because through the Christian community we have met Jesus Christ, heard his word of invitation, and responded to him in faith. We assemble together at Mass in order to speak our faith over again in community, and, by speaking it, to renew and deepen it. We do not come together to meet Christ as if he were absent from the rest of our lives. We come together to deepen our awareness of, and commitment to, the action of His Spirit in the whole of our lives at every moment.

We come together to acknowledge the work of the Spirit in us, to offer thanks, to celebrate.

"People in love make signs of love and celebrate their love for the dual purpose of expressing and deepening that love. We too must express in signs our faith in Christ and each other, our love for Christ and for each other, or they will die. We need to celebrate.

"We may not feel like celebrating on this or that Sunday, even though we are called by the Church's law to do so. Our faith does not always permeate our feelings. But this is the function of signs in the Church: to give bodily expression to faith, to transform our fragile awareness of Christ's presence in the dark of our daily isolation into a joyful, integral experience of his liberating action in the solidarity of the celebrating community.

"From this it is clear that the manner in which the church celebrates the liturgy has an effect on the faith of men. Good celebrations foster and nourish faith. Poor celebrations weaken and destroy faith."

Those words are likely to arouse unease in most people, making so strong a connection between faith and feeling. Another writer puts it this way.

"People should come away (from the celebration of the Mass or any sacrament) with a sense of having experienced their faith, of having felt that they believe in Jesus, of having celebrated something."   (Ledogar p.18)

We are therefore faced with the problem of the validity of emotion and feeling in prayer and faith. One clue to be kept in mind when approaching this area is that line in the decree which says that "the sacred signs must be experienced as intensely as possible." It is in the experience of eating and drinking that the presence of the Risen Lord is perceived; it is in the experience of the hand pressed on your head, that remnant of the hug of love, that we know too of God's loving forgiveness. Sacraments are effective through a human experience. In the case of music, of singing together, there is also something of this experience achieved.

By it we know that among all of us who sing together there is a oneness in faith in the Risen Lord, and in that experience of oneness, we know that he is present, making us one, living in us. Christ is present in the people gathered.

Victor White, in his commentary on St. Thomas' letter to Brother John, explains St. Thomas' thought as follows:

"A vigorous sense-life is not merely, for the student, a condescending concession to his 'lower nature,' it is a necessity for his studies themselves. Although 'in divinis est imaginatio omnio relinquenda' (In Boeth.de Trin. VI.2), our abstract thought itself becomes a mere game with paper money, concepts corresponding to no real wealth, if it is based upon no real experience of our own. Particularly so in Theology, for sensible symbol and metaphor are the principal medium of God's Self Revelation (S.T.I.i.9)."
("Sensible signs" mean the sacraments; "metaphors" mean principally sacred scripture.)

So when we are saying the Creed together each week it is not done primarily to enable us to flick down through the main headings of our doctrinal beliefs, the headings of the catechism; it is more about experiencing our unity of faith. That is also again why singing, as a ritual, singing a recognised tune like Credo III – Credo in unum Deum – can have much more importance than even the words; it has an immediate effect of evoking that sense of knowing "here, I belong."

"Whatever music is good at, it is not good at transmitting clear and distinct Cartesian ideas. Sing the Creed and you soft-pedal the theology," but you highlight the sense of identity of the group. And, of course, to soft-pedal the theology is not always a bad thing. To quote Aristotle, "persons undergoing initiation are not expected to gain knowledge, but an experience and a disposition." Ritual and liturgy are not primarily about passing on information. They are about an experience of being a Christian, an experience of being united in faith with this group of people, and of affirming that faith with one's whole being.

More important still, in the liturgy, that faith is strengthened in you by the living Christ who makes us one. Cardinal Knox said at the 1977 Synod: "To view liturgy as principally a vehicle for catechisis would destroy the whole liturgical movement," because it destroys prayer – and "bad liturgy weakens or kills faith." If you turn liturgy into a catechism class you do not help faith to grow; it is bad liturgy, and bad liturgy kills faith.

Sing "Credo In Unum Deum" and it triggers off all the learned responses of the past and encapsulates one's whole sense of belonging to the body of believers. It catches our whole lifetime of being a Christian, along with the heritage we received from those who went before us.

It is exactly similar to the example we had earlier, of looking at the Cross, wordlessly, which can sum up our whole understanding of Christ and the Father's love for us. Looking at the Cross can evoke the certainty that no matter how insoluble things may seem to us, the Father's love is not in contradiction to any pain that we, or Christ, might have suffered.

In *Worship* (Jan. 1979) Eric Routley made the apt statement:

"I often say to people that the reason why we must take special care over the music of our hymns is that they will be sung by people who are not musical, who are uncritical, who may not have time or ability to notice that this isn't what they really mean. By the same token I would say of the language of hymns and prayers that it is especially important to get it right because it is not being attended to critically, or paused on, or argued over. When somebody tells us that some of our customary language implies and actually engenders wrong attitudes, then I think this is a signal we must all take seriously. But those who draw our attention to such a state of things need not expect that everything they charge will be accepted without proof. I venture to say here that at one point they are entirely right, and at another, quite wrong."

However, we must also keep in mind that even though we acknowledge the validity of emotion, and its expression in liturgy, we must not embarrass other people by getting them to sing or say words which really do not suit them, or coercing them to sing music which does not suit this occasion. "O Mother I could weep for mirth . . .", just does not go with teenagers, even though we all know that there are times when joy does well over into tears. Therefore, we have to be very discerning if we are to decide what sort of words, what sort of hymns, can act as an expression of the unity in faith, as it is possessed by this particular group. A small group of young people, you might say, sniffing their way back into the Church, needs quite different music from a crowded church on Sunday (early Mass, main Mass, evening Mass) or a huge rally at the show-grounds.

For the small group which is a formal group, such as a religious community, Gregorian chant had a special kind of effect. The faith of such people is known to one another, and so they can use a more stylised or sophisticated ritual, like plain chant. It quite readily achieved the ability to enter into prayer, even to very deep prayer, without embarrassment or religious selfconsciousness. Such a group regards it as completely normal to pray together. But we must remember that plain chant is a spiritually sophisticated ritual (as sophisticated as the illuminations in the Book of Kells); it is a learned signal, which can lead those who are accustomed to it right into the area of contemplative prayer.

At the other end of the scale, it is all too easy for hymns to be emotionally dishonest, and to use them to force a crowd, who are not at all in the mood for it, to announce that religion is "Joy." Hymns with emotionally inappropriate overtones are an easy trap. Tunes which have associations with totally secular events, dance music or pop music, act as a counter-signal to the call of the gospel. "Only artistically sound music will be effective in the long run. To admit the cheap, the trite, the musical cliché often found in popular songs on the grounds of instant liturgy is to cheapen the liturgy, to expose it to ridicule, and to invite failure." (American Bishops' Directory on Music.)

Imperceptively we have moved around to hymns, so we must at this point face up to the concrete situation. Participation, almost everywhere, means singing four hymns – entrance, offertory, communion, recessional. Even in regard to singing, this, of course, is not what the Constitution on the Liturgy and the subsequent documents recommended. The four hymn Mass leads directly to the major flaw that is criticised in Ralph Keifer's article: "music and maximum involvement in the peripheral parts, dull flatness at what should be the high points." Generally, what we succeed in doing is to exhaust the congregation, and this is particularly so in school Masses and children's Masses, so that the readings and the Eucharistic Prayer become a marked anticlimax. People are over-stimulated in the unimportant parts, and bored by the main parts.

In practice, what the decree envisages is that music starts from the centre outwards. If there is going to be singing, it should first be used in the Eucharistic Prayer. Normally, one should not use all the opportunities for singing as outlined in the decree. It is excellent to sing a lot for a big occasion, but hardly advisable as a daily routine, or even as a weekly routine. One must, therefore, make a choice.

The Decree on Music, May 1967, indicates the priorities to be observed in choosing what parts to sing.

1. The first "degree of active participation" (what a horrible phrase), suggests the singing of the Sanctus, Acclamation, Amen, Lord's Prayer. Incidentally, for the sake of non-singers, and also for a chance to be meditative, I usually prefer to recite the Our Father. Otherwise, non-singers feel terribly excluded. The first degree of participation is nearly all within the Eucharistic Prayer.

2. The second degree, adds Kyrie, Gloria, Creed, Agnus Dei.

3.   And only in stage 3 (which is regarded as being only for more special occasions, or for a congregation that is well able to take a lot of singing), does it suggest that entrance song, psalm, alleluia, communion song, should be sung.

You see, it is exactly the opposite to the 1958 Four-Hymn-Mass. How did they arrive at such a conclusion?

1.   The obvious reason is that singing is used to enhance and emphasise the crucial parts, especially the Eucharistic Prayer, or the Acclamation before the gospel.

2.   The most usual way for a crowd or a group to respond as a unit is by a shout or a cheer or an acclamation. The Sanctus, the Acclamation, the Amen, Kyrie, alleluia, are all basically acclamations. (This principle is being recognised more explicitly in the more recently composed Eucharistic Prayers, which include acclamations that are repeated frequently.) This is why people so readily sing the Eucharistic acclamations.

3.   The decree also calls on a mysterious principle (s.6-7), which speaks of parts of the Mass "which of their nature demand to be sung." It does not make very clear where they get this principle, or how to apply it. Indications are, that it primarily points to these great acclamations, which should punctuate the Mass – Sanctus, alleluia, Amen, etc. How stupid one would feel if one tried to recite the National Anthem. For a start, one would not even be able to remember the second line of it if it was not sung. Worse still, imagine being asked to talk "hip hip hurray."

In recognition of the principle, the later documents tells us that if, for example, the alleluia is not sung, it need not be recited. The American Bishops' Directive to Catholic Publishers, 1975, takes this principle to its obvious conclusion when it points out that the entrance verse, alleluia, communion verse, etc. must not even be printed in Mass books for the laity, unless musical text is given. If, of its nature it demands to be sung, then it should be omitted if it is not sung. To tell the truth, the greatest irritant to most congregations at Mass, even though they probably would not be able to pinpoint it, is the endless recitation of snippets of texts, one after another, which have nothing to do with each other. But nearly always, such snippets are merely the text of parts which ought to have been sung.

The most obvious example is that unfortunate piece, the *Responsorial Psalm*. It is everyone's experience that one has to blot out everything else from one's mind in order to remember that wretched response. Obviously, it is something which was meant to be sung, and if it is not sung, either the psalm itself should be slowly recited by the whole congregation, or by some individual, while all listen. The term "Responsorial Psalm" is not the special name for this part of the text. It is simply the "psalm." "Responsorial" refers merely to the way in which the psalm is said or sung. The psalm may be dealt with in any number of ways. One person may read it; one person may sing it; the whole congregation may recite it in unison, or each side of the church may read alternate stanzas, or it may be sung responsorially, where the congregation sing a short phrase like: "His goodness shall follow me . . .", and then the soloist sings the verse, or the whole congregation can sing it. But the truth is, as one writer has put it, "the Responsorial Psalm is the worst example of liturgical archaism in the whole of the new liturgy," a hangover from a style of singing common in monastic choirs.

Perhaps, as an aside, it might be useful to clarify the distinction that is made between an antiphon and a response. At face value, as one looks at the texts of responses and antiphons in the liturgical book, it is not possible to see any difference; each is just a single sentence or phrase. The terms "antiphon" and "response" refer to two ways of singing; they are musicological terms, and they really have no application whatever in "recited liturgy." The original difference is that, in singing the psalms responsorially, the main group of people sang a short phrase to a simple melody. Then the soloist went on to sing the verses of the psalm, on his own, to a more complicated melody. The people sang the response repeatedly at the end of each stanza. Now, with antiphons, things happened the other way round. In an antiphon, the text had a complicated musical setting, and so the choir sang the antiphon (as we had in the old Gregorian chants – fairly long, fairly complicated), and then the congregation sang the psalm to some simple melody.

The two words, as musicological terms, indicate the degree of complexity of the musical setting. If one is in fact singing everything to simple music, both the "response" and the psalm, it is pure archaism to demand a distinction, or indeed to indicate a preference for "responsorial" singing. The people are capable of singing the psalm themselves. Furthermore, in the American Bishops' directives for publishers, they insist that not only is the music to be given for the response, or else the response is not to be printed; also the words of the psalm itself must be printed. The congregation must be able to see what the psalm is, what the words are, and if opportune, they can sing the psalm too, to the usually uncomplicated music now given for the singing of the psalm.

But whichever way you go, it is nonsense just to recite scraps of four or five words. They are the texts for musical settings, and reading them is sheer nonsense. Let us stop the confusing term "responsorial psalm." It is simply the psalm.

Although the psalm is recommended to be sung only in the "third degree of participation" this is the important sung part of the liturgy of the Word. Yet it is still more important that the people first catch the sense of the psalms as prayers. People need to acquire a familiarity with them by reciting them together. It is also then much easier to make the transition to singing later on. Even at the level of choral technique, a choir or congregation cannot sing psalms well if they are not first familiar with the speech-rhythms of the particular translation. It is very simple then to use any of the well known settings: Gelineau, Bevonet, Murray, etc.

In summary –

1. Our singing should be from the centre outwards, from the Eucharistic Prayer outwards. If you are going to have singing, priority is given to these acclamations which are nearly all within the liturgy of the Eucharist.

Acclamations are the most useful and normal way of involving people who are not accustomed to prolonged, hearty congregational singing at Mass. As a beginning it will be found quite effective to use one of the Eucharistic acclamations repeatedly throughout the Mass, sung as the Gospel acclamation; at the Alleluia; again as the Memorial acclamation; incorporated into the Great Amen, as an expansion of the Great Amen; as an introduction to the Communion rite or as a communion verse. Eucharistic acclamations can be used to punctuate the whole Mass.

2. We need more acclamations, and to use repetitive acclamations, which, like the Eucharistic acclamation, capture our whole faith, summarise our whole sense of being Christians: "Dying you destroyed our death . . ." Such acclamations could punctuate both the liturgy of the word and the liturgy of Eucharist.

Lastly, one has to issue a word of warning to organists and choir-masters. The numerous decrees and papal pronouncements in praise of religious music do not necessarily prove that the hymns or music you have chosen are an appropriate part of ritual for this particular congregation. We have to be able to distinguish praise for religious music as such and approval of the appropriateness of this particular music for this group at this time. Because a hymn has been written by Palestrina or Bach or Ray Repp it does not necessarily mean that it will capture for these people the core of their sense of being one in Christ, their sense of identity. Who would have ever thought that he would hear an Irishman, who presumes to a little knowledge of theology and of music, praising "Hail Glorious St. Patrick" as being, on certain occasions, the most appropriate music. All the attempts in recent years to produce more elegant poetry or more worthy music for our national hymn have fallen on barren ground. The other, banal as it is, is for us the most deeply felt signal of the sacred – signal to us, of who we are.

The American Bishops' Directive on Music, 1972, offers a totally new division of music in the liturgy, which throws everything into a new light. They do not say that this is the order of priorities, but it offers an important new method of classification.

First: The five acclamations:
1. IIcre they change the 1967 decree slightly. The first acclamation they give is the Alleluia, not the acclamation after the Gospel: Praise to you Lord Jesus Christ.
2. Sanctus.
3. Eucharistic acclamation or the Memorial acclamation.
4. Great Amen.
5. The doxology after the Our Father: For Yours is the Kingdom . . . By implication they suggest it is more important to sing this doxology than to sing the Our Father. It is an acclamation, which "of its nature demands to be sung," and which in fact, if given a chance, people most readily sing.

Second: The two processional songs:
Entrance song.
Communion song, i.e. during the Communion procession.

Third: The psalm (not necessarily sung responsorially).

Fourth: The ordinary chants: Kyrie, Gloria, Creed, Our Father, Lamb of God. The Agnus Dei may be sung by the choir, as meditatie music.

Fifth: The supplementary songs:
a) – possible singing at Preparation of Gifts, by the choir, to accompany that procession;
b) – possibly a hymn after Communion;

c) – a recessional. Their comment on the recessional is worth noting. "A recessional song has never been an official part of the Roman Liturgy. Hence musicians are free to plan music which provides an appropriate closing for the liturgy. A song is a possible choice. However, if the people have sung a song after communion, it may be advisable to use only an instrumental or choir recessional."

Much could be written on the way in which music can refine our spiritual instincts. St. Augustine was very sure of this, and we cannot easily contradict him when he said: "Bis orat qui cantat," one who sings, prays twice over. There is no doubt that music can calm our agitation, can help our meditation, can inspire us. If you allow yourself to be drawn into it, it becomes more wholeheartedly, unselfconsciously, involving.

But still, we must keep to the forefront of our minds that *Noise*, singing, speaking, or even the gentle grunt, are not pleasant additions to make the Mass more entertaining. They are integral parts of ritual or liturgy. They are integral parts of the sacrament, in which Christ's presence is experienced and we are redeemed; here one comes to know "Who I am" – the body of Christ.

6 DEVOTION

THE NEED for devotion in the liturgy may, at first sight, seem quite opposite to the stress so far given to the ritual elements of the liturgy. To most people, ritual, by definition, is not spontaneous. Therefore, they assume that ritual is divorced from any feeling or emotion, even the valid emotions experienced in prayer. I would suspect that many would think that liturgy ought to be rather formal, and free of emotion: personal devotion being something one indulged in, in private, but which should not obtrude in public worship. Yet, no-one can deny that there is a quality of devotion which is needed at Mass, and in recent years it is fairly rare to find it.

The word "need" is not used here in the sense that it is something we demand like spoiled children, but rather, something which religion needs, because it is of the essence of religion. In the lovely phrase Ralph Keifer uses, devotion is about "basking" in the love of God, being able to sit there and allow the fact that God loves us to seep into every crevice of our consciousness.

The most fundamental statement in all theology is that statement made in the first chapter of the Book of Genesis: "God saw what he had made, and it was good." God loved it; God loves us. So much of Christian behaviour is dependent on that as its foundation. So much of the writing of the New Testament takes this for granted as its starting point: "If God so much loved you, you therefore must love one another." You see, St. John takes it for granted that the fundamental Christian insight is the awareness that God loved you first. The first Christian insight, mystical intuition, is not that God exists, but that God loves. With this comes the awareness too that we are loveable. Consequently, believing this, believing it with the very depths of our being, we are capable of recognising the loveableness and the goodness that God puts into others. Love for one another is the consequence of our awareness of first being loved by God.

Devotion is the quality of being able to sit gratefully in the presence of that love, in the way that you like to sit, without needing to talk, in the presence of others who love you, or whom you love.

The New Covenant is God's renewal of his assurance of his love for us. So when the Eucharist is called the "Sacrament of the New Covenant," we are saying that the Mass is the high point at which the Christian experiences this being loved anew by God. And therefore, to want to sit on in the marvel of it, that is, to have devotion, is the one quality which should be evoked immediately, and always, by our celebration of the Mass.

The previous chapters have tried to take away some of the things which distract us from that marvellous fact: overemphasis on the introductory rites, or the rite for the preparation of the gifts, or an inappropriate use of music. The present chapter will deal with some of the characteristics, both of mind and performance, which destroy devotion; and then how should we foster devotion more in our celebration of the Mass.

Without doubt, the first cause of defect is still the residue of legalism – a phobia about getting everything right. We are not to be blamed for this. One of the characteristics of Catholic liturgy for the last couple of hundred years, since the Council of Trent, has been its tendency to overemphasise legal points, getting things done properly. The rubrics (the regulations directing the priest at Mass) were so detailed that it was actually prescribed in what order the candles should be lit on the altar; it prescribed which arm the priest should first put into the sleeve of the alb. Everything was catered for legally. The legal niceties of ceremonial etiquette are beyond imagining – all of which bound the priest under pain of sin – prescribing everything from the colour of his socks to the angle at which he held his arms in prayer, or bowed his head. Only now are we escaping from that mentality of an excessive emphasis on legal points in prayer.

As yet we are still quite unaccustomed to using the word "ritual" in its wider sense as used by anthropologists, in which it refers to every form of human communication. To us, the word "ritual" is heavily loaded with the idea of detailed prescriptions of court-etiquette, every part of which is laid down by law. But the very term "liturgical law" is to some degree an anomaly. Ritual by legal prescription is as unnatural as Esperanto. True ritual grows out of customs which have now become heavy with meaning. In liturgy, the legal point is never the important point.

Prayer is what is of importance in liturgy; and prayer is essentially about devotion. The liturgy of the Word and the liturgy of the Eucharist are, above all, the points at which God's loving covenant, his loving way of dealing with men and women, is brought before us, and we are enabled to see that that is the way in which he has been dealing with each detail of our individual lives too. Paragraph 7 of the Constitution on the Liturgy, speaks of Christ's presence in the priest presiding, in the people gathered, in the Word spoken and the sacred meal shared. Prayer is about being in the presence of God, in the presence of Christ. In prayer one is aware of how much one is loved, aware that it is good to be here, with the Lord.

However, we must now also acknowledge that when the Constitution on the Liturgy, and the subsequent reforms, were being drawn up, they over-emphasised "meaning," "intelligibility," "clarity of thought" as essentials of liturgy. "The rites should be distinguished by a noble simplicity, they should be within the people's power of comprehension, they should normally require no extra explanation." "They must be clearly expressed, understood with ease." All those phrases in that section of the Constitution were concerned with clarity and intelligibility. Yet, of course, the most important things in life can rarely be put into words clearly. So often we spoil love by trying to talk about it. Therefore, because of that slightly excessive emphasis on intelligibility, it was inevitable that for some years after the initial reforms we failed to see that in trying to make it all simple and intelligible, we were working in opposition to the nature of ritual as such. True ritual evokes feelings, instincts, emotions, which convey, in ways that words never could, the awareness of God's presence and of God's love.

Even though one of the decrees does say "the sacred symbols must be experienced as intensely as possible," our first reading of the Constitution, in 1964, led all of us to think that what it demanded was the vernacular language and intelligibility. We hardly noticed the other elements.

Archbishop Weakland, writing in *Worship* in 1975, says that it was only after ten years that an assessment could be made. No major damage has been done by a slight deviation for a few years. However, because of this stress on intelligibility, many of the qualities which had characterised our devotions in the past, were stiffled by an over-emphasis on words. It was insisted that we must not have unnecessary repetition; logic and clarity were at a premium. But, of course, one of the main characteristics of devotion, and of all love-talk, is that it goes round in circles, it repeats itself, it uses mixed metaphors, and it is never primarily involved in getting information across.

Really, not until now, was it possible to see where our defect originated, or that there were defects there at all. There is no point in blaming ourselves for having taken a slightly wrong track. No great harm has been done.

When we come to consider the question of devotion, we must first recollect the qualities of the great devotional exercises of the past: Benediction, Stations of the Cross, visits to the Blessed Sacrament. There was a quality of warmth, a quality of timelessness about them. Things did not have to be done with the utmost hurry. Texts were nearly always the same, for devotion does not get tired of repetition. In "devotions" variety is not necessarily the spice of life. This is not due to any obligation in law to follow an unchanging formula. It is just that devotion, like love, grows best in an atmosphere of familiar homeliness. It is something of that quality of devotion, the thing that made our devotions of such great help to the ordinary Christian, that we must now recapture, and allow to be experienced again, within the Mass.

Distortion of another sort arose when those who were reforming the liturgy chose the model on which the new liturgy was to be shaped. The model they chose was the classroom. This is not to say that there is anything intrinsically wrong with classrooms, there is an obvious place for them; but prayer is something different. Those who drew up the new rites worked on the model of the classroom in the sense that they assumed that liturgy and classrooms are about the same thing; passing on information, teaching, getting ideas across. As Ralph Keifer notes, the Creed was not originally a method of proving our orthodoxy, it was a kind of lyrical song in which we sang about our commitment to Christ. Thinking of liturgy in terms of a classroom led us to see the priest first as a teacher; the liturgy of the Word was information about God; the sermon as extra information about God. Even the prayers of the faithful tended to be extra bits of information, minor correction to one another, or even information to be passed on to the Almighty. As Herbert McCabe put it: Prayers seemed to take the form: "Lord, as you may have noticed in this morning's editorial in the Herald . . . ." When everything is concerned with information we do lose sight of the fact that prayer is about devotion; prayer is about being in God's presence, experiencing his presence.

What then are the principal vehicles for devotion in this sense? The answer, though not immediately obvious to everyone, is: the sacred symbols, the priest presiding, the Word spoken, the people gathered, the Eucharistic meal shared. These are the ways in which Christ's presence is experienced in the liturgy. Yet, in truth, these are not the elements which spring to mind when we think of that past atmosphere of devotion. Rather, it was candles lighting before our Lady's statue, incense burning at Benediction, litanies, familiar hymns, and prayers which had become the vehicle for deeply felt, but quite valid emotion. One has to admit that the build-up to the renewal of baptismal vows by candle-light at the end of the parish mission in the old days worked better as ritual, and seemed less contrived than the present attempt to use candles at the Easter ceremonies. The dynamics of the mission-ceremony were just better ritual than our present awkward lighting of the Easter fire, followed by a procession which goes nowhere, and is no more than a short shuffle back into our pews. The candle-light procession at Lourdes, or other shrines, is just good natural ritual. There is something primitively satisfying about walking in a group through the dark, by candle-light. However, since we have got rid of all these processions, for Christ the King, Corpus Christi, or the May Processions, we are quite unpractised at making the processions on Palm Sunday and Easter Night feel real or, quite literally, satisfying.

Curiously, one has to add that the lack of discipline is one of the qualities working strongly against the success of much liturgy, even in its ability to be devotional. People who do not really know what to do next, or what to expect next, can never be at ease and therefore, open and receptive. Ritual requires a degree of formality (although it has to guard especially against becoming a gym-display). It is the element of formality which transforms a crocodile of people sauntering along the road, into a procession. A procession is ritual, and it effects us, and a person identifies himself with the ritual by conforming to whatever minimum requirements are needed. One of the reasons why so much liturgy at present is so lacking in devotion is that we have not yet plucked up enough courage to indicate how to act, how to take part. Our reaction against rigid legalism and rubricism has made us afraid to ask for any formality at all; and without that there can be no such thing as ritual, or liturgy, or, as a consequence, devotion.

It is fitting that candles, incense and processions and the like should again find their place in our prayer. Yet even in the past there was no doubt that they merely surrounded the central focus of our awareness of God's presence, either in the Blessed Sacrament, or in other devotional practices. It is important therefore, that we again learn how to connect the concept of "devotion" with Christ's presence as experienced in the Word, in the priest and in the Eucharist.

To take the single example of the liturgy of the Word, this means that scripture has to come to be seen as the account of other men's experience of his presence. The gospels are the account of what the writer felt it was like to be in the presence of Christ. As St. John says in 1 John 1:1-4: "Something which has existed since the beginning, that we have heard, and we have seen with our own eyes; that we have watched and touched with our hands: the Word, who is life – this is our subject." Scripture is simply the account of this writer's experience of being close to God, of seeing God's hand at work, above all, of seeing God in Jesus the Lord, the Risen Lord. They give us the record of their experience of God – whether it be an Old Testament prophet, or an evangelist, or St. Paul, or the early Christian community itself. That record, the seventy-two books of the bible, is, in turn, normative in guiding us towards a sharing of their experience, here and now. They point out the direction for us to look, if we too are to come to their experience of God's presence, that is, to share their devotion.

But those writings are also, secondarily, the yardstick by which we assess the validity of whatever experience we ourselves may now have. Therefore, while conveying to us their experience of God's presence in Christ, the sacred writers of scripture also teach us to be able to distinguish real from false experience, to be able to distinguish real sorrow for our errors and faults from an attack of indigestion on the "morning after the night before." As the Fontana edition of *The Psalms* puts it in its introductions to Psalm 29: "The devil was sick, the devil a monk would be. The devil was well, the devil a monk was he." There is some truth in this. Good health has its own unconscious arrogance and is even accompanied sometimes by a deceptive feeling of holiness. Sickness opens our eyes: we look back on our lives and are frightened by the selfishness of our motives. When we recover, our conduct may not improve but at least we may be grateful for our recovery in our prayers.

"I said to myself in my good fortune:

"Nothing will ever disturb me.

Your favour had set me on a mountain fastness,

    then you hid your face and I was put to confusion."

It is all too easy when it is a nice day and you are feeling good, to imagine that that is holiness. You only need to stub your toe for the illusion to shatter disastrously. In this way, the psalms teach us to distinguish real experience of God's presence from illusion.

The liturgy of the Word is the ordinary and most constant way in which we are brought into God's presence, that is, we come to have devotion. As suggested in Chapter 1, one needs to learn to take away some phrase in the Mass readings that sums up the experience of God's presence as told to us by this prophet or this evangelist, and linger on it. Perhaps it is the scene of Mary pouring the rich ointment on the feet of Christ; the symbol of the complete "wastefulness" of love. Love is "useless," in the best sense of the word; it does not try to achieve results, it is not functional. Judas' reaction was to ask why the ointment had not been sold and the money put to practical purposes, or given to the poor. Love does not work that way: "Love is not calculating."

After Mass on any particular day, we should take away with us something like this, then later on we should spend time on it, learning to linger on it, not working out meditations, or examples for tomorrow's classes, just being there in the wonder of it until it warms our hearts. Gradually it will attune us to listen to the readings with even a greater sensitivity, to hear how someone else – another of the sacred writers – at some other point in the life of Jesus, became aware too of God's loving presence, came to live in that state of devotion which is prayer.

We started this section by noting how intelligibility had been the standard and the classroom had been the model for liturgical reform. On the contrary, symbols are the real way in which ritual or liturgy works. I have given the example of one such symbol, Sacred Scripture. The same must be applied to all the other symbols, both in the Mass and in the other sacraments. In each case one sees that clarity and intelligiblity are, by no means, the primary way in which the experience of God's presence, devotion, is evoked.

The Council of Trent used an altogether different model for describing liturgy. Trent first set about legally defining what liturgy was. This was the first attempt to use legality as the norm for defining prayer. Trent defined liturgy as the official worship of the Church. As a result, all other prayers of Christians together were thereby defined as non-liturgy. When it was said, then, to be non-liturgy, that quickly came to be interpreted that this was not the Church praying. For example, when the parish priest and two hundred parishioners were making the Stations of the Cross together in Lent, that was not the Church praying. But in reality, as Jesus says: whenever two or three are gathered in my name there am I in the midst of them.

Fundamentally, wherever the Church in fact is praying, there is liturgy. Therefore, the severe distinction which the Council of Trent drew between liturgy and the popular devotion tended to disenfranchise nine-tenths of the prayer life of most Christians. Curiously enough, it held that when a priest was saying the Office on his own, sitting in front of the head-lamps of his car at 11:00 p.m., that was liturgy; but when a packed congregation was making the Stations together, that was not the Church praying, it was not liturgy.

The distinction was being attempted to be drawn on the basis of legalism. Over the centuries that legalism became further convoluted by describing the Divine Office in terms of certain people being given a mandate to pray in the name of the Church. All this gave undue emphasis to the bits called "liturgy"; it underestimated the elements called "devotion." This, in turn, fed back into the Mass itself, so that it came to be taken almost as a sign of weakness of faith to want the Mass to be devotional. The thing worked "ex opere operato," and it made no difference whether you understood it or not, whether you felt any devotion or not. It made no difference at all that thousands of nuns spent every day saying the Office in Latin. Legally they were defined as "the Church praying" and, like the effect of the Word of God in the story of Creation – "and it was so." By legal "fiat," the Church was declared to have prayed, whether or not anyone felt devotion; whether or not anyone had come to know the essence of prayer; being the presence of God.

Vatican II's Constitution on the Liturgy, began the process of setting aside legal definition as the model on which to define and shape liturgy. However, it is in some more recent writings that the real change of ground becomes more apparent. Some commentators speak not of the four presences of Christ in the liturgy, but five: they add the presence of Christ in the community after they have shared the Eucharist together. We experience Christ's presence also in one another's devotion, in one another's faith. And in that too, we contact Christ, we experience the real presence. It is not only in the sanctity of Mary and Lazarus and Martha, or in the words of John or Paul, but in each other, that we experience the real presence.

Remember again, that for St. Thomas, the words "Real Presence" meant the presence of Christ in us, his people. The "Mystical Body," for St. Thomas, or the Sacramental Presence, was the presence under the appearance of bread and wine, transubstantiation. For St. Thomas, transubstantiation was quite secondary to the real presence. It was not until this century that these two terms got mixed up and transposed. The real presence is that Christ, and through Christ, the Trinity, lives in us. Sacraments are the means to that reality; and sacraments are, in the strict sense, merely sacraments. The real presence is Christ's presence in his Body, the people of God.

That is what these recent writers are referring to when they speak of this fifth way in which Christ's presence is experienced in the community after they have celebrated the Eucharist together.

One of our great tasks from here on is to learn to bring back into the liturgy that devotion, that contemplativeness, which is at the heart of all prayer, and which is also one of the crucial points at which Christ's presence is known. Here, the Christian most fully, and almost endlessly, basks in the presence of the Risen Lord, sits there just "admiring God," as Ralph Keifer so well puts it.

The introductory rites of the Mass need then, to become an invitation, a call, into that presence of Christ. They need to have far less stress on information, or themes or moral reprimands. As most people agree, our liturgy is far too wordy. We are punch-drunk by verbal battering after the first twenty minutes, and therefore, switch off.

From this however, one may not conclude that devotion has to be brief. We may not be ready for it ourselves, but we cannot dismiss the devotion that enables the whole of Eastern Christendom to spend from three-and-a-half to five hours celebrating the Mass. This same devotion allows some charismatic meetings to spend two to three hours just "being in God's presence." It becomes clear then, that devotion is not concerned with passing on extra information about God, but about making them aware of his loving presence. The longer that lasts, the better it is. Timelessness is one of its characteristic qualities. Along with that, we must become aware of one's privilege of being able to rub shoulders with each other who share this great destiny, of being the Body of Christ.

We are privileged to know about Christ. We are not saying that we are better than people who do not know, or who know little of him. But we are privileged. Therefore, there is an assurance in the way in which we can pray in the prayers of the faithful, the assurance in which we can confide the needs of our world to the Lord whom we know loves us, loves his people, loves his world. Prayer of petition then becomes a normal consequence of our devotion.

Therefore, what is needed is that we learn how to be devout together, how to share our prayer together, without imagining that we are going to embarrass one another, without too readily accusing ourselves or others of being emotional, or dismissing it all as rather unsafe.

Indeed, one has to guard against excessive emotion. Emotion can never become the measuring rod by which we decide whether or not God is present. But our gladness in being together with one another in the presence of the Lord is one of the qualities that must gradually pervade our gathering to celebrate the Mass together. And in that gladness, in that devotion itself, we come to know what it is to be the Body of Christ, the awareness that it is good to be here.

That, I think, is far more important in the introductory rites than the slightly unfortunate phrase used in the present introduction to the penitential rite: To prepare ourselves to celebrate the sacred mysteries, let us call to mind our sins. As one writer puts it: "The revelation of God's loving presence is made to be a disclosure of new ways to experience inadequacy and guilt, and bear, somehow, divine responsibility for the deterioration of the universe, without the power to bring life, or share divine joy." The invitation to celebrate the Mass must not be made to sound like an officious discouragement. It is about knowing of God's loving presence, knowing that even failure, like the failure of the Cross, becomes the point at which God's presence is known. As a friend said to me once when I was complaining about things going wrong: "failure is not always a sign of lack of success." And every year, since then, we have used those words as the motto for our Holy Week ceremonies. "Failure is not always a sign of lack of success." It is the paradox of the Death and Resurrection. Even our sins must not induce the discouragement which makes one reluctant even to celebrate the Eucharist. We must come, glad to be there, for Christ is there, and he heals all ills.

The Council of Trent approached liturgy from the point of legal definition and rubrical propriety. Because it wished to stress the objective effectiveness of the sacraments it tended to soft-pedal the subjective faith and devotion of the individual. In fact, to want devotion in the Mass was almost taken to be a sign that one did not believe that the sacrament worked in its own right. As a result, in the following centuries man's fundamental need for devotion began to find expression in the many extra-liturgical "devotions" so common until twenty years ago. Meanwhile liturgy was deprived of one of its essential qualities.

Out of Vatican II derives the bible service, which was really an extension of the classroom model. It also tended to be too informationally orientated; it lacked the warmth; it lacked that delight in praising God, just in singing, as all of us instinctively felt at Benediction, or in saying the Divine Praises, as people still feel in a charismatic meeting. I think it is because of its obsession with information and themes that bible services never got off the ground.

Youth Masses tended to produce other models. These fall roughly into two groups. There was the youth Mass which was the expression of some anti-establishment feeling, sometimes typified by the singing of that most awful hymn "Narrow-minded people in a narrow-minded street," which referred to all them out there, except us nice people in here. There was the other kind of youth Mass which attempted to say that religion is fun, fun, fun: "honk if you love Jesus."

Other groups were concerned with social action. For them, the function of liturgy was "conscientisation," making people aware of social issues. Ralph Keifer mentions: "I can't count the number of times I've been to a baptism which to me seemed more like an induction service into an ethical society than into the loving presence of the redeeming Lord . . . Where the candle is given to the newly baptised person with admonitions to go out and be a light to the world, without any mention that baptism and the candle might first be about Christ's light shining in the world of this individual."

Some years ago, a priest in Ireland, visiting a school, asked the children what was a saint. Eventually one little boy gave the answer, referring to the stained glass windows in church: "It is a man the light shines through." The light of baptism is far more about that than about demonstrating before the White House.

Another attempt to produce a form of liturgy, which recovered devotion, has been the charismatic Mass. Unfortunately, because of the dynamics of a charismatic meeting, the priest presiding tends to be overshadowed; others become the liturgical leaders. The main symbols of Catholic liturgy are again subjected to ritual imbalance, to some degree. Yet this is truly an attempt to do what we must all learn to do more effectively. It tries to put something back into the Mass which we all sense we had lost, something of that gladness, something of that sense of the presence of God, of the mystery of God's loving presence.

The conclusion which is forced on us is that liturgy can never be drawn up at a committee meeting. It cannot be drawn up by a committee of liturgical experts in Rome, nor, for that matter by a parish liturgy committee meeting either. It is something in which the dynamics of this particular group has to be allowed its own expression; it cannot be altogether pre-determined or rail-roaded. But certainly a parish liturgy committee can greatly help if it has a balanced understanding of the meaning of ritual and prayer.

The over-emphasis on information, the lack of emphasis on devotion, gives us the clear indicator of how we can begin again to touch the tiller, to readjust the balance, for it is largely a question of balance, not a question of exclusive alternatives. Of course, we need information about God; of course, we need to hear how John and Paul tell of their experience of God. Ultimately what we are trying to achieve is a balance between these elements.

Liturgy must come back to the sense of God's timeless beauty, and some element of that timelessness in our admiring him must be part of our daily lives. The essence of devotion, therefore, is the experience of being in this relationship of friendship with God; a friendship which is the covenant. And that is, ultimately, why the Eucharist itself is defined as the sacrament of the New Covenant.

Mass without devotion, Mass that tends to become a classroom, has missed the point of being in the friendship and loving care of God.

7 WHAT IS PARTICIPATION?

THE QUESTION which forms the title of this chapter might well be expanded to ask "who participates in what"? To this it is all too simple to assume the answer that participation is obviously about taking an active part in singing or responses. By now however, it must surely be clear that that answer will not do.

Liturgy is ritual; and a particular ritual is used by a special group or community or culture, to express its understanding of life, to strengthen that understanding and pass it on. At the same time, a group uses ritual to affirm, or re-affirm, the role of the various people in the group, and the relationships that bind them together as a community. These are the two functions of ritual: celebrating and passing on one's understanding of life, and establishing what is the role of various people in relationship to each other.

Long ago, in Psalm 49, God made it quite clear that liturgy was not required because God had a neurotic need to be worshipped. He told the Jews that he did not want more bullocks or rams offered in sacrifice. They all belonged to him anyhow. Amos 5:23 adds a detail more applicable to ourselves: "I loathe the strumming of your guitars." He does not need our hymn-singing, any more than he needs our bullocks. Whatever the obligation to go to Mass on Sunday may be about, it is certainly not the same as the Sunday afternoon excursion to see grandfather in the Old Folks' Home, when all the children are paraded in their Sunday best, and each one does his party-piece. Participation in the liturgy is not something we do to please a slightly neurotic God.

Who then is liturgy for? Who participates? Two quite different answers have been given to this question recently by two very respectable authorities. Aidan Kavanagh, in the article from *Doctrine & Life* (July, 1973) says: "First I suggest that we priests must deepen our awareness – or recover it if we have lost it – that our primary ministry is not to the world in general but to our communities of faith in particular." But in his Encyclical of 1975 on Evangelisation, paragraph 51, Pope Paul states that "announcing the Kingdom for the first time to those who have never heard of Christ has been, ever since the morning of Pentecost, the fundamental programme which the Church has taken on as received from her divine Founder."

Who then is liturgy for? Is it a service for the community of faith, or is it aimed at announcing the gospel to those who have never heard it?

Without doubt the liturgy is the supreme announcement of the good news: Let us proclaim the mystery of faith: "Christ had died, Christ is risen, Christ will come again." At whatever level it occurs, this announcing the gospel always carries with it a call to repentance. Conversion is initially a process which takes place over many years, culminating eventually in the catechumenate and the liturgy of baptism and the Eucharist, and entry into the Christian community. But the whole Christian life is about conversion, so that every celebration of the Mass is a call to renewal. The dilemma can therefore be restated: is it our primary task to call to conversion those who have never heard of Christ, or is the Mass essentially concerned with deepening the conversion of those who already believe?

Aidan Kavanagh makes the point that many of the younger clergy and people in America seem to assume that the Eucharist can, and must, be made meaningful to the unconverted – to anyone, so to speak, who just happens to walk in off the street, or grows up into it as a baptised pagan. Aidan Kavanagh is, therefore, using the word "unconverted" in the sense of totally uninitiated or, perhaps better, uninterested. However, liturgy, ritual of any sort, speaks only to someone who shares something of the world view of that particular group or culture. Christian liturgy, the Mass, can convey meaning only to someone who has come to see that the world makes sense in terms of the death and resurrection of Our Lord. It cannot make sense to any-one who simply walks in off the street. This of course is why Rahner is so vehemently opposed to televising the Mass. Ritual will almost necessarily seem absurd to one who does not share the world view, the faith, of those for whom that ritual was fashioned.

To whom then is the liturgy directed? Neo-pagans, bap-tised pagans, baptised catechumens, the community of faith? I strongly hold that liturgy, especially the Mass, can have meaning only within the community of faith. It is because we are always watering things down, with an eye on the "man-in-the-pew" whom we assume to be only a baptised pagan, that we end up challenging no-one, en-riching no-one. We need to have far more confidence that the People of God are capable of hearing the Word of God, of understanding it and receiving it. Or, rather, put it the other way round: the Word of God is capable of making itself understood and of penetrating minds. As Isaiah says 55:10: "Yes, as the rain and the snow come down from the heavens and do not return without watering the earth, making it yield and giving growth to provide seed for the sower and bread for the eating, so the word that goes from my mouth does not return to me empty, without carrying out my will and succeeding in what it was sent to do." God's word, like the Creative Word in Genesis, speaks, and it achieves what it says. But if we perpetually water it down,

we blunt the edge of the two-edged sword of the Word
of God.

There is the added assumption which we have carried
over from the 19th century London Mission Society tech-
niques, that one cannot start making Christians until one
has made people clean, respectable citizens. Preaching
therefore, often never gets around to announcing the death
and resurrection of Christ; its moralising often has little
more content than the 19th century Victorian "salvation by
soap and water – cleanliness is next to Godliness."

The most fruitful starting point in this discussion is
offered by J. Murphy O'Connor in *Community & Eucharist
in First Corinthians*. Father Murphy O'Connor makes two
points. He speaks first of St. Paul's notion of the community: the community is Christ; and Christ is the community. First of all, for St. Paul, you do not start with a
whole lot of individuals as it were, whom you bind together.
The community is Christ, Christ is the community, and you
are absorbed into Christ, you are drawn up into Christ.
The community exists before you. The community, the
Body of Christ, exists before the individuals who are subsequently made part of it.

Father Murphy O'Connor's second point is that Paul set
himself the task of creating an alternative environment in
which the individual could survive as a Christian. In the
words of Aidan Kavanagh, the catechumenate is about
conversion – and how to survive it.

What then is the relationship of a person within the
Christian community to the outside world? "The individual
who rejects the value system of his society is necessarily
treated as an outsider, deprived of any real capacity to effect
change. Being a Christian is inevitably to become a marginal
person," pushed out onto the rim of society. From one end
of the world to the other, people who are taking an active
role in being Christian are being gaoled and persecuted.
People who are different, as Jesus himself was, become

marked men. The Christian will inevitably find himself a martyr. "Virtually insurmountable obstacles are put in the way of his living out the values he cherishes. His existence is absorbed in a struggle against an all-pervasive and relentless pressure."

Therefore, Paul saw his task as the creation of an alternative environment in which a Christian could survive. So Paul was forced to envisage an environment in which the individual would not only be exempt from the destructive pressures of bad example, but would be subject to the inspiration of good example, in a group in which all could say "imitate me as I am an imitator of Christ."

In his commentary on the epistle to the Philippians, Murphy O'Connor says that St. Paul, in speaking to any community where he himself had preached, always uses the phrase: "be imitators of me as I am of Christ." But in writing to a church where he was himself unknown, Paul instructs Christians to imitate those who live according to the example given them by Christ. Paul saw that without such living models within a community, the community inevitably slumped into legalism to achieve conformity of morals. Normally the Christian life is achieved through the imitation of living models. As an aside, one might add this also underlines the importance of reading lives of the saints as other example of such living models of Christianity. The Christian community cannot survive without its models, it cannot survive without its history, without someone to look up to, or rather, someone who draws us up, almost in spite of ourselves.

For Paul therefore, the whole community is the basic Christian reality. Not only is its mode of existence willed by the Creator, but it is the only practical and concrete means whereby an individual is rescued from the false orientation of a fallen world. Only in an authentically Christian community is the individual free to become as God intended, is he free of the pressures which would make it impossible for him to live as a Christian. Without community, totally committed to the living of Christian values, there is no genuine freedom. The freedom to grow, to be fully human, as Christ is fully human, is founded exclusively on the effectiveness of the protection against the compulsion of sin, which the believing community gives to those who belong to it. It is impossible to live solitarily in the imitation of Christ.

So what community does is, in fact, to create an environment where a person can live by faith and hope and love. Can live by faith, that is, where all is seen as having meaning in terms of Christ's death and resurrection. Where we stand back from the values of the world, in other words, we fast. Where with compassion we serve those whom the world would crush. The Christian can live this life because he is protected, not by a false protection, but by that necessary strengthening without which no individual can be Christlike. He lives in the environment where it becomes possible to live by Christian values. He lives there not merely because the community gives him good example, and backs him up, but because the community is Christ; the community gives Christ. In him we live and move and have our being.

Here of course, we were so accustomed to speaking of the Mystical Body that we do water down dreadfully the literalness with which St. Paul saw the relationship of the individual Christian to Christ. We are the Body of Christ. These remarks obviously act as a strong corrective to the usual assumptions about what is meant by a "sense of community." Consider the following:

Constitution Par. 42. Efforts must be made to encourage a sense of community within the parish, above all in the communal celebration of the Sunday Mass.
Instruction on the Eucharist.
Par. 13. For no Christian community can be built up unless it has as its basis and pivot the celebration of the

Holy Eucharist. It is from this, therefore, that any attempt to form a community must begin.

Par. 18. An awareness of the local and universal Church community is to be fostered.

In the celebration of the Eucharist, a sense of community should be encouraged. Each person will then feel himself united with his brethren in the communion of the Church, local and universal, and even in a way with all men. In the Sacrifice of the Mass, in fact, Christ offers Himself for the salvation of the entire world. The Congregation of the faithful is both type and sign of the union of the whole human race in Christ its head.

It is very easy to misinterpret all these references. If by a "sense of community" one means a great feeling of chumminess, camaraderie, being man-to-man, then in this sense, liturgy does not create community. Ritual creates nothing. Ritual does not create community; ritual is something that a community already existing uses. So one cannot say "liturgy creates community." Communities use ritual, use liturgy. If however, by a sense of community one means the sense of knowing that we who share in this liturgy have here no abiding city, that we as Christians will always, necessarily, be living by values which the world cannot understand, then in this sense, liturgy can strengthen the sense of our assimilation of those values; it can bind us together in a shared faith and vision. More correctly, one should say again, it draws us individuals into the community which is Christ.

At times, of course, non-believers and the neo-pagan world will in fact see how we live, and although they do not understand our motives or our reasons, they will often sense that Christ's answer is best. Sometimes they will imitate us and support us but, as the Old Testament, especially the prophets, so constantly beat home, it is foolish to make alliances with them or to feel that we have been proved right because some point which we have championed has at last become government policy. As Jesus says: "I depend on no man."

Being a Christian, or rather, becoming a Christian, involves taking on an outlook and values that are simply not just "sweet reason and common sense." The Death and Resurrection are no recipe for a quiet life. Making that outlook one's own calls for a constant process of repentance and of personal conversion. To the world this will always seem foolishness.

Liturgy, therefore, is concerned with that conversion, with taking on the values of Christ; and then with surviving it. "Baptism is the way the Eucharist begins, and the Eucharist is the way baptism is sustained" (Kavanagh p.349). Conversion and survival: we can survive the conversion celebrated in baptism because of the community which nourishes us, which absorbs us into the Body of Christ.

At the present day, however, we are in some danger of falling between two stools. Having lost the adult catechumenate, we are now, instead, expecting all this conversion process to be achieved from our mutual participation in the Sunday Mass. The faithful, the baptised catechumen, the baptised pagan, are all there together at Sunday Mass, and one hour's liturgy is expected to achieve conversion for all of them. This is a completely unrealistic, unobtainable and inappropriate expectation. It is foolish to imagine that one hour's liturgy can achieve conversion for all these totally different states of spiritual development.

This brings us therefore, to consider for a short time, the question of the adult catechumenate. The restoration of the adult catechumenate is one of the most interesting of all the liturgical reforms. From now on, the standard by which baptism is understood is not infant baptism but the baptism of an adult. What is envisaged in the new rite of baptism, is that the person to be baptised, or received into the community, spends two to three years as a catechumen. The purpose of the catechumenate is to produce "someone who has something to repent of and something to celebrate, and who knows how to do both in common .... This conversion is achieved less by being lectured at (or having a correspondence course from a Catholic Enquiry Centre) than by living in close association with people who fast and pray and share their faith and their service of others with regular ease and flair."

A catechumen therefore, over a three-year period, is drawn into the life of faith, that is, the world view, of the community. Over an extended period like that, he is enabled to see how the world makes sense for the Christian in terms of the Cross and Resurrection. He is then led to see all that that implies, at every sort of practical level. Secondly, he is drawn into the life of prayer of the community. St. Thomas calls prayer the "voice of hope," the awareness that "In God we trust," and that by God's power and presence this whole impossible programme becomes possible; that it is possible to live by such a vision of life, understood in terms of Christ's death and resurrection. Further, that love is possible, and within this Christian community, love is possible even among the unlikely. "See those Christians, how they love one another."

Over this period of two or three years therefore, the catechumen is drawn into the life of faith, the vision; the life of prayer, which is the whole source of hope, and into the loving service of others, which forms the life of this community.

The adult catechumenate is proposed in the new rite as the norm by which all baptism is to be understood. The baptism of an infant child demands that the parents and their immediate small community have to go through this renewal, this reconversion and recommitment of themselves. In this sense the baptism of an infant has more to do with the parents than it has to do with the child. This re-conversion and re-dedication of the parents, drawing them into the community which is Christ, ensures that this child will be reared in the environment St. Paul envisages, where it is protected from sin, and the world, by the living presence and values of Christ's love.

One of our pastoral problems at present is that even an adult convert is still given instructions, and then dropped into the middle of a parish where he knows nobody, and nobody knows him. The adult convert often suffers from extreme loneliness, totally contrary to what St. Paul envisaged that conversion is about or Paul's idea of the indispensable function of the Christian community in providing an alternative environment in which the new Christian can survive.

The question we must ask then is: to what extent can the Sunday Mass be such a call to conversion, enabling people like ourselves, who already are Christian and baptised and faithful, to deepen our repentance? Can Sunday Mass establish the kind of community that is capable of sharing its prayer, sharing its faith, sharing its love? Is it expecting more that can be achieved from the Mass to think that it can give us a strong sense that we are going to be living by very different values, and that this fasting is the common vocation of us all? Fasting here does not merely refer to such things as the Friday Fast for Justice. Fasting is being used here in a much more basic sense, its strict Christian sense of turning away from those values of the world and living by other values. To what extent can we, and do we, as a Christian community, support each other in that essential stance of being Christian, and how much of that support can come to us through a Sunday Mass? Or, is "being a Christian" still an impossibly solitary job for us, mere individuals. Is the best we can hope for that the Sunday Mass will give us the strength to go on, on our own? St. Paul implies that the liturgy must help us, must be the place that forms that environment in which we can survive our conversion. Because none of us can survive as Christians if that sense of community is not there to support us.

How then can we make the Sunday Mass to be that kind of help for us? How can we come to be aware that we are not alone in this stance we take, whether it be about family life or honesty at work or just being more generous than a "calculating co-operativeness." These are the values we must feel strengthened in, through having celebrated Mass together.

Obviously, not all of us can do everything. We cannot all be involved in every kind of ministry of mercy. Many of the things we do, are done quite silently, no-one else hardly knowing – not letting your left hand know what your right hand is doing. Hardly anyone is aware of the kind of work many of us are doing. A certain degree of secrecy and hiddenness is essential to the doing of many tasks. But somewhere behind all this one must have the sense that others, other Christians, understand why we are willing to endure this difficulty, even to endure it with joy and gladness. As Thomas More says in *A Man For All Seasons:*

"I am faint when I think of the worst that they may do to me. But worse than that would be to go, with you not understanding why I go."

Lady Alice: "I don't!"

More: "Alice, if you can tell me that you understand, I think I can make a good death, if I have to."

Alice: "I don't understand. I don't believe this had to happen."

More: "If you say that, Alice, I don't see how I'm to face it."

We need the sense that there are others who share these values which are in contradiction to the world, and who therefore will understand. In sharing those values, we belong together to the Body of Christ. That sense is indispensable if we are to survive as Christians.

Secondly, it is not enough that the community merely understands. The Christian community performs a greater function still. The community indicates for a person that the way of acting that he has undertaken is a truly Christian way of acting. They affirm that this is the way a Christian lives. In this sense they affirm what you are doing, they authenticate it. This is how the discernment of the Spirit is done for us. The community senses, and somehow enables us to know that it senses, that what we are doing is truly done in the Spirit of Christ. It is not a matter of public applause, nor even of any noticeable participation in our effort, but the *sensus fidelium*, the instinct which the Christian possesses, not so much as an individual, as a community, for recognising that Christ is there. This *sensus fidelium* affirms for the individual the correctness of his instinct in following Christ.

The major question therefore, arising from this chapter, is: how can the liturgy perform that task, of being an adequate expression of such a community's life and purpose, and of the community's responsibility to the individual? The readings in the Mass, the psalm, the homily, the prayers of the faithful, the remembrance of the death and resurrection of the Lord, the communion, the devotedness that we experience together, these are the factors that establish for us our awareness of being the community in Christ.

Participation in the liturgy is firstly about that particular community of faith. No matter how weak one's own faith may be, the community, in celebrating its faith, strengthens our faith. And by its very strength, it enables those who are merely baptised catechumens, or even baptised pagans, to perceive that there is a power greater than Solomon, a wisdom greater than Solomon, here.

Participation is about this kind of experience of the community of faith. If this is seen, then our whole approach to planning celebrations of the Eucharist will gradually be transformed. In time, it will enable us to be less afraid of being outspokenly Christian with each other when we celebrate the Mass. As a consequence, too, we will become capable of being outspokenly Christian in word and action in the face of a world whose values we are rejecting, and which will inevitably reject us, as it rejected Christ.

Participation in the liturgy means that, no matter what stage of conversion or re-conversion we are at, we are being called again to move ahead, and then, strengthened in our vision, of our understanding of life lived in terms of the Death and Resurrection, we are confirmed in our conviction that such a life is possible – the virtue of hope; and we are strengthened in our love, by which such a service is done to others as Christ has done for us. Those three things: faith shared, hope revived and love strengthened, are achieved in us through the liturgy of the Word and the liturgy of the Eucharist.

TENTATIVE CONCLUSIONS

I therefore, would conclude that liturgy, in particular the Mass, is aimed at the community of faith. It is a renewed call to ever more demanding conversion (perhaps demanding is an ugly word); God's love calling us to assimilate more completely the values summed up in the Cross and Resurrection. At the same time, the Mass, the liturgy, establishes that kind of community which protects the Christian from the pressure of sin. It assures us in the words of Our Lord: "take courage, I have overcome the world . . . fear not, little flock . . . I am with you through all days, until the end of time." I am convinced that something of this can indeed be experienced in the community celebrating the Mass together.

My second conclusion is that it would probably be much more appropriate to take the various stages of the adult catechumenate as the liturgical model for many groups to whom we now offer the Mass as the only liturgical option – groups who are de facto only at various levels of the catechumenate. They have not yet come to faith, they are in the process of becoming believers. This does not mean that we must deprive them of the Mass, by immediate edict. But it is not being helpful to offer them only those parts of the Church's liturgy for which they are not yet ready, to offer them only those parts of the liturgy which require a mature faith, the world view and ethos, the faith, hope and love of a committed Christian. Without doubt this has important implications for many school groups and groups of young people.

Yves Congar discusses how the Council of Trent attempted to define the Church in legal terms, and then outlined the legal requirements for constituting membership of the Church, and also the consequent duties of members.

The Constitution on the Church, in Vatican II, totally avoids the use of the words "members of the Church." It avoided the legal definition. Congar therefore, points out the inappropriateness of imposing legal obligations on people whom one cannot legally define. The Christian's duties do not derive from the notions of positive law. One does not therefore, immediately tell people not to go to Mass. However, it is important that they know that the reason we go to Mass is not because Canon Law obliges us. Further, let it be stressed again, that the appropriate kind of liturgy for a person who is de facto only a catechumen, or de facto still a pagan, although he may have been baptised, is probably some part of the liturgy for the adult catechumenate, not, to use the old phrase, the Mass of the Faithful.

Thirdly, a community needs living models, and it also needs its heroes, its past, its saints, its traditions. The living model has two tasks to do. The catechist (or the guru, it is more or less the same idea), is not merely a model that is imitated at a distance. He is primarily someone who knows how to initiate others into the kind of outlook on life that this community possesses.

The catechist is one who knows how to bring a person from what we take for granted to be the obvious way of solving questions at the human level, to the point where he sees his life in terms of the Cross and Resurrection. The obvious "reasonable" answers to the questions, perhaps about family life, or work, are subtly changed. A reversal of life-understanding is brought about in the "convert" over a two or three year period, as he absorbs this Christian mind from the catechist.

The catechist, secondly, initiates the person into prayer. Prayer does two things. First, by prayer, the individual interiorises the Christian outlook. Then, through prayer, we know that this whole impossible programme is possible by the strength of Christ, who is present at the heart of this whole mystery, who is present, and gives life to this community, who is the Christian community.

Thirdly, the catechist initiates people into an understanding of Christian mercy, a compassion that differen-
tiates the women who stood at the foot of the Cross from
the soldier who offered the sponge full of vinegar. Christian
mercy is quite different from State Social Services.

As Thomas Merton said: "The monk is compassionate
in proportion as he is less practical and less successful,
because the job of being a success in a competitive society
leaves no time for compassion."

My fourth conclusion is that it is the community of faith,
prayer and love that makes it possible for the individual
to withstand sin. That is, the community breathes the Spirit
of Christ into each one of us. We are the vehicle by which
the Spirit is given to each other, the Spirit by which the
individual is christened, becomes another Christ.

Fifthly, concerning preaching: although this applies
primarily to priests, it has also a lot to do with the expectations of the congregation. It is not the job of the preacher
to point out in detail the practical implications for every
particular situation. Preaching offers us the Christian map
of life; and it makes us aware that the map is largely the
journey through the desert. It is most common to find
people who have written themselves off spiritually, imagining that they are no longer on the map, because they are
somehow spiritually in the desert. Preaching gives the map,
the kind of route along which the Christian passes, the
route that is described either in the desert journey of the
Jews, or in the journey of Jesus up to Jerusalem. As the
individual himself sees the map more clearly, he will
recognise in what direction he must move as a Christian.

The most striking example I can give of this is the work
of an Auckland architect who writes a weekly column in the
paper. In one of his articles written at Easter-time, he
described how he had found an old ship's mast on the city
dump. The mast had subsequently been used as a flag-pole,
and now he has made it the centre-column of a spiral stair-
case in his house. But he pointed out that he could not notch

the mast, in order to slot in the steps; instead, he grooved each step so that it clung to the mast, for you must not so use the material things of the world that you destroy the possibility that they can rise again to a new life. So as one puts the broken glass into one bin, and the tins into another, and the bio-degradables into another for re-cycling, one is every day being reminded of the Resurrection. The seed, dying and rising, finds its parallel in a world of tin-cans and bottles; and the resurrection of Christ can change our outlook even on our way of using the world's material resources. This example is of course not a dogmatic statement on which all Christians must agree, but it is an insight into his own job that only an architect could see, as he dwelt on the meaning of a particular mystery of the faith preached in the liturgy.

It is not the priest's task to discover how the gospel applies to the details of each one's professional work and personal life. If the liturgy of the Word presents the map of Christian life, of conversion, then the Spirit will show each individual how it applies to him. We must not cramp the Spirit. God's Word can enlighten individual hearts much more accurately and readily than our little bits of practical shrewdness or even pastoral theology. As Pope John said to religious superiors: "The purpose of all authority in the Church is to make men responsive to the Holy Spirit."

Let us ask the question again: What is Participation? Who participates in what? By now it must be clear that the issue is far deeper than deciding about hymns or about buying a new electric organ. The question really is, how is this community enabled, in this celebration of the Mass, to experience conversion, and become the Body of Christ. And secondly, how do we enable these Christians to survive their conversion; how do we create a community which protects them from the false pressure of non-Christian values, and on the contrary, leads them to the full maturity that Christ offers. That is what participation envisages.

8 THE LITURGY OF THE WORD

IN THE PREVIOUS CHAPTERS we have been looking at the various elements which make up ritual or liturgy. In the light of this discussion we must now attempt an analysis of the Mass, with its constitutive parts, the liturgy of the Word and the liturgy of the Eucharist.

There are three ways in which we can approach the question of the liturgy of the Word:

1. The liturgy of the Word as sacrament and ritual; as a sacrament in its own right.
2. The lectionary, its structure and contents.
3. The training courses for readers; and the spiritual formation needed if a true ministry of the Word is to be evoked among those who now act as readers.

THE LITURGY OF THE WORD AS SACRAMENT

It is important once more to stress that we are dealing here with a real presence of Christ; and, secondly, that we are dealing with prayer, with being in the presence in Christ. As was said in the previous chapter, through this reading we are being allowed to enter into the experience of God's presence, as these sacred writers recorded their own experience of it for us. They recorded their call into the presence of God. It was a call to conversion, or a call to faith. The manner in which that Christian experience comes to us is exactly parallel to the way in which ritual is used in any culture.

Integrally bound up with its rituals are a community's myths. The word "myth" in this context does not mean that something is historically untrue. A myth is a story, whether a piece of history or of legend, which sums up the sense of identity of this particular group. For the Maoris it may be the stories of the canoes, for a Frenchman, it is the French Revolution. The French Revolution is not only an historical fact, it is also what anthropologists would call a myth. The characteristic of a myth is that the incident, whether taken from history or legend, is transposed on to another level where it now encapsulates the whole sense of identity of that particular group or culture. The word myth, therefore, is not used in contradistinction, or opposition, to the word "history." Myth is concerned with something much more profound than mere historical fact. Like the gospel parables, a myth catches a people's whole philosophy of life.

Part of the task of ritual is to pass on the community's myths, by re-enacting them in some way. A procession to mark Bastile Day in France, or Waitangi Day in New Zealand is a ritual of such importance that even those who are opposed to what it symbolizes instinctively focus on Waitangi Day celebrations, and once more express that opposition in a ritual like cutting down of the flag-pole.

Recent writers have been less afraid to use the word myth, in its strict technical sense, when referring to the key events of Jewish and Christian religion. The titles of Andrew Greeley's three books are *The Sinai Myth, The Jesus Myth* and *The Mary Myth.* He is not denying that any of this is historical. He is recognising how, in strictly anthropological terms, these particular stories sum up our sense of being Christian; they enable us to enter into the experience of being a Christian.

The Christian world view can be summed up by saying that "life makes sense in terms of the death and resurrection of Jesus." Still, a single page of scripture cannot be neglected if we are to catch the endless depths of what is now a most familiar summary of our faith: Christ has died, Christ is risen, Christ will come again.

The reading of scripture is the reading of our history. It tells the story of the People of God in the Old Testament, first gathered from the descendants of Abraham, and the story of the New People of God, brought into being by Jesus. It is exactly like the telling of the genealogy of a tribe within Maori or Samoan culture. In these cultures a man comes to know who he is through the ritual of reciting his genealogy. The ritual of reading scripture establishes our identity as God's people. The reading of scripture brings us the awareness of who we are. It does not merely provide information about our family history; it enables us to know it experientially, as Peter and John and Paul knew it. Paul states it briefly in Romans 8: "The spirit you received . . . is the spirit of sons, and it makes us cry out, 'Abba, Father.'" That is who I am; I am one who knows that, in Jesus, I am a child of God, our heavenly Father.

The liturgy of the Word is ritual, it is sacrament. Therefore, the same principle applies to the liturgy of the Word as to all the sacraments: the symbols must be experienced as intensely as possible. An initial source of error at this stage is to think that the symbol is just the text, or at most, the book, the bible. The symbol, the sacred sign by which Christ is sacramentally present in the liturgy of the Word is the living voice, speaking. There is a major difference to be noted between reading and meditating on scripture privately, and scripture as read to us in the liturgy. In the liturgy, it is a real presence, a sacramental presence of Christ.

You may draw a parallel with the distinction we make between the text of a Shakespearian play and drama. to read the text is not the experience of drama. Nor is reading a musical score the experience of hearing a symphony. So you cannot say that the mere text of scripture is a sacrament or ritual. The sacrament is always the living voice speaking.

That, incidentially, is why it is so important to listen, rather than to do what is normal within most of the Protestant tradition, where each person brings his own bible, and follows the text. The sacrament is not just the words on the page, it is the voice speaking to you.

Furthermore, that voice is the symbol or sacrament not only of Christ speaking to us, but it is also the symbol of the Church. The scripture is given to us by being handed on to us by generations of Christians whose own lives are "the living gospel." These words pass on John's or Paul's experience of God's presence in Christ; they also carry the assurance that generations of Christians have found it to be true.

Scripture, as read to us in church, has something in common with poetry. W. H. Andrew's comment is enlightening here. He says that when you read a mediocre poem you say to yourself: "Yes, I've felt like that – my heart jumps up when I behold a rainbow in the sky." But when you read a great poem, you say: "That will never look the same again." This is supremely true of the Word of God, proclaimed within the sacramental rite, Christ speaks through the human voice talking to us, penetrates our hearts, and enables us to experience life in such a way that it will indeed never look the same again.

RITUAL ANALYSIS OF LITURGY OF THE WORD

The simplest way to analyse the liturgy of the Word as ritual is to ask the question: who says what, and where and why? Who speaks, or who does not speak?, what are various people doing? What are they saying? where are they?

Where are they? In this regard it should be noted that the Third Instruction, paragraph 2b, states that the liturgy of the Word, and the liturgy of the Eucharist, must not be celebrated in different places or at different times. As a general rule it forbids the practice of having the readings in one room, and then moving to the dining room (or the chapel) for the liturgy of the Eucharist. The two parts make up the one sacrament, they are the one proclamation of God's saving word. The two parts are not to be separated in time or place. No matter what sacrament is being celebrated, it contains a liturgy of the Word, and this liturgy of the Word is an integral part of the sacraments. "I absolve you" is said by the same voice, the voice of Christ, that spoke to you in the scriptures. The same voice that called you to repentance in the reading, later proclaims your freedom from sin. The readings are not just information to prepare us for the real sacrament; it is all part of the living presence, by which Christ speaks, Christ calls, Christ heals, Christ gives us life. To have the readings in a hall, and then to move to the chapel for the Eucharist could easily convey the idea that only the Eucharist is the real sacrament – therefore the insistence that the whole sacramental rite should be celebrated in the same place.

The Directory for Masses for Children, shows the obvious exceptions to this rule. It recommends that children should have a liturgy of the Word for themselves, in a different place, while the adult community is celebrating this part of the Mass in church. But it is because children are in various stages of the catechumenate that they need to celebrate the liturgy of the Word on their own.

The question about where the liturgy of the Word is celebrated conceals a number of major issues. The congregation who are to listen are just as important as the words to be read. One must ask therefore, what does this building do to a congregation. There is something architecturally wrong with the lay-out of a church if people stay at the back pew. To remain outside the circle of participants is a "ritual" way of saying: "I want to remain apart from the assembly; I'll stay just here, as an observer." In this case the person is not consenting to be part of the listening assembly. As a result, it is impossible to involve that person in the readings. This is not necessarily because of bad will on a person's part. Usually it is due to architectural details which are operating against the dynamics of ritual. For example, rows and rows of pews act like a series of hurdles, over which visually one has to leap, before getting to the sanctuary. Most of us are just intimidated by it, and stop short inside the back door. It is the architect's task to provide the kind of flexibility that enables a building to be easily adapted to large or small groups. We would rightly feel indignant if we came to a reception centre for a function to which fifty guests had been invited, and found that empty tables and chairs for two hundred cluttered the rest of the room. Not infrequently, churches are unsatisfactory for liturgy because the architect was unaware that he was to provide a space for ritual. Too often a church is conceived in terms of a monument, or, at best, a theatre.

Similarly, any modern building which needs a loudspeaker system must be regarded as architecturally a failure. On the other hand, if loudspeakers are in use, they need to be monitored for every separate voice. Monitoring a loudspeaker system is just as necessary and constant a task in a church as being the organist. No other professional group would use sound systems without someone at the controls throughout. It is ridiculous to suggest that volume controls can be fixed permanently, and will suit everyone, tall or short, loud or timid, who approaches the lectern.

The first symbol to come to mind when thinking of the liturgy of the Word is the lectionary or the bible. The respect shown to it, as a permanent symbol, speaks to the whole congregation.

This is further emphasised if the bible is brought in, in procession, if candles, and even incense, are used at the lectern. Needless to say, these latter suggestions are secondary, but they do alert people to the fact that the readings are the first high-point in the Mass. To read the lesson at Mass from the back page of the Catholic newspaper, or a leaflet missal, is not only undignified, but it deprives the congregation of this whole set of signals which make the people aware that this is the climax of the first part of the Mass.

Next we can ask the question: who speaks? It is easy to list off the answer: the priest, the readers, the one who leads the psalm, the leaders of the prayers of the faithful. The whole congregation too has its time of speaking, its time of reflecting prayerfully. In the liturgy of the Word, there is a rhythm of people speaking, listening, responding. In this way they enable each other to share in their experience of God's word and their response to God's word. in their silence and devotion, in their alertness to listen, they communicate to one another, that Christ is present in these words spoken to them.

Readers

A major task facing us at present is to help readers see that they are fulfilling a truly sacramental role. At this point they are the vehicle by which Christ is present to this congregation. God's word and presence is communicated in an exactly parallel way to the role of the special ministers in distributing communion. The reader's function is in no way a lesser function than that of the special minister.

Probably one of the most forceful means of awakening this sense of the importance of the readers' role is the use of some public ceremonial of official installation of readers, as we already have for the installation of special ministers of communion. It might be recomended that the readers should receive a blessing from the priest at every Mass, such as the words: "May the Lord be in your heart and on your lips to proclaim his message of salvation." The formal installation and blessing for special ministers makes them aware of the particular privilege of distributing Holy Communion. But they also become intensely aware of their responsibility, not only to handle the Blessed Eucharist with dignity, but also the responsibility for evoking from the community the kind of valuing of the Blessed Sacrament that that rite of official installation achieved for them.

The following news report from the *Aukland Star* illustrates the point:

"The magic that the *moko* worked during the making of 'The Governor' was one of the most astonishing aspects of the TV1 production, say the crews who filmed the episodes (like tomorrow night's) featuring Maori chiefs in major roles.

"The *moko*, or facial tatoo was an indication of the social standing of the bearer, various lines indicating whether a man was a warrior, or an orator, and how much *mana* he had.

"It was distinctly noticeable, during make-up sessions for 'The Governor' how the bearing of the Maori actors visibly changed as the *moko* progressed.

"Thus, when the actors finally emerged, wearing the *korowai*, carrying the *mere* and bearing a *moko*, they carried themselves with a dignity in line with their rank.

"In the old days, the application of the *moko* was a long and painful process involving two and three pronged bone chisels, tapped into the flesh with a mallet. The wounds were then coloured with vegetable dyes, soot, or animal fats – in fact, any number of crude but effective colourants."

If grease-paint can do that to a man, the sacramental rites of the Church achieve incomparably more. Ritual, in the strict sense, achieves this awareness of one's role, whether it be the ritual by which a tribal leader is installed, or the Church rituals, by which a special minister is installed, or by which, I suggest, readers too need to be installed, if they are to realise what is their immense importance. As a consequence of the preparation and ceremony of installation for special ministers, the task is undertaken with great seriousness. The need for a parallel installation for readers becomes apparent. Readers will then become aware that they have a further responsibility towards all those to whom they proclaim the Word; their duty need not stop just at reading the few lines of the Sunday reading. Rather, that initial task becomes the starting point for a whole ministry of the Word within this community. In time, they may well become leaders of groups reading scripture, or prayer groups. Ultimately they become the catechists in a community, those who know how to share their faith and their prayer.

A further point about readers is that they fulfill, what the Constitution and the decrees call "a genuine liturgical role." Readers may therefore, always receive communion under both kinds, like the special ministers, at every Mass, even if the congregation at large are not permitted to do so, either on this particular occasion, or in this particular diocese. The general law of the Church allows communion under both kinds to all who fulfill a genuine liturgical role. If the reader is, in fact, singled out in this way, it too emphasises in the eyes of the whole congregation, his great standing.

The Homily

We come now to the homily, the essential and characteristic task of the priest in presiding at the liturgy of the Word. If another priest or a deacon is present, the presiding priest should not read the gospel. The homily also needs to be re-integrated into its whole ritual context: it is not just more information about God. In a homily a priest shares his faith. The priest allows others to enter into his experience of Christ's presence, as it has come to him in listening to the Word of God, which he and the people together have heard.

One must conclude, therefore, that all sermons, like all good writing, philosophical or political or religious, are to some extent always autobiographical. The words one subsequently uses may seem quite impersonal, but their value depends on the speaker's experience of the truth. Otherwise, words are only paper money which corresponds to no real wealth. The opening verse of St.John's Epistle is the yardstick for all preaching.

The homily should never be just theological formulae being repeated or further elaborated. It must always convey the faith as the priest has experienced it; the experience of Christ's presence, of Christ's death and resurrection. In the truthfulness of his sharing of that experience, the homilist enables others to perceive too that Christ is manifesting himself to them.

The Creed

At this point, we have to come full circle, and we must recognise that the Creeds originally were doing for religion what the poet does for other areas of man's experience. The poet looks at something, and catches some meaning there which the rest of us had not noticed; he catches some insight into human existence. The statements of the Creed are exactly like that; they capture, and encapsulate, an experience of God's presence. Therefore, our reciting of the Creed, like our reading of scripture, must always link back to that experience; and it must lead us, and others, to sharing that experience. Even the Creed, therefore, is always about the presence of God, who leads us, who enlightens us, who is living in us, and in whom we live. "I believe in God, the Father Almighty," is not a theological formula. It is first of all some individual's statement of his whole perception of life transformed by his awareness that God is.

The difficulty arises from the fact that in English we have no equivalent to the Latin words *Credo in Deum*. The Latin verb *credo* changes its meaning according to the case of the noun which follows it. Credo deum: means I believe that there is an "object" called God. Credo deo: means I believe God. That it, I believe what God says. Credo in deum: in Latin "in" followed by the accusative case expresses motion towards another, so this phrase means literally "I believe into God." It conveys the idea not just of information accepted, but the sense of entrusting oneself into the hands of another person whose fidelity I trust. The phrase might best be translated by saying "I entrust myself into the hands of the one God who is the Father Almighty, creator of heaven and earth."

Credo in unum Deum sums up the experience of some great saint of the early Church, whoever it was that first coined the phrase. Some poet or mystic in those words found the perfect way of expressing his act of faith, his giving of himself into the hands of the Father whose love is endless. The Creed is a kind of litany of the ways in which the saints of the early Church experienced God's presence. The purpose of that litany is to lead all of us into sharing the splendour of those points of vision and enlightenment. The Creed is therefore about the presence of God who loves us and enlightens us. It is not just a check-list of dogmatic orthodoxy.

Prayers of the Faithful

If the readings, the homily, the Creed have been leading them into the presence of God, the congregation, in the prayers of the faithful, will then be able to share their faith and prayer. The prayers of intercession will express how they too know what has been talked about, that they also give their lives into the hands of God, and that they are aware how all this impossible programme of overcoming the world can be achieved in God. "Let us with confidence then approach the throne of grace, knowing that we shall have mercy from him in our time of need." (Heb 4:6)

The liturgy of the Word as ritual is totally about sharing the experience of the presence of God, as that is conveyed to us by the writers of scripture, by the attentiveness, devotion and faith of the others present, by the homily, the Creed, and by the confidence with which we can pray together in the prayers of intercession.

THE LECTIONARY

One cannot help but be puzzled at the way in which the gospel readings for the Sundays in the three-year cycle in the lectionary have been chosen. An initial glance might seem to show that Matthew's Gospel is read in Year 1, Mark in Year 2 and Luke in Year 3, with John being read mostly during Lent and Easter. But this simple solution does not stand up to analysis. How are we to spread thirteen chapters of Mark, twenty-three chapters of Luke and twenty-five chapters of Matthew with equal adequacy over the thirty-three Sundays of the year, plus Advent and some of Lent? In Year 1, there are, in all, forty Sundays when Matthew is used; in Year 2, thirty-two Sundays when Mark is used; in Year 3, forty-two Sundays when Luke is used. (Luke Chapter 15 is used twice and the Infancy Narrative is used on the Feast of the Holy Family.) One must also keep in mind that two of these Sundays will be superseded every year by Pentecost and Trinity Sunday, as well as others which are displaced by major feasts which fall on a Sunday. The many "special days" for peace, vocations, etc, when alternative readings are recommended, reduce the figure still more. On top of that there are always two or three Sundays dropped between where we left off before Lent and where we pick up again after Trinity Sunday. The compilers seem to have operated on a calendar which had fifty-six Sundays in the year!

On what system then were these necessarily limited selections made; and having been made, the question must be asked, do they give, with any adequacy, an opportunity to present the distinctive thought of each of the evangelists? It would certainly have been helpful if the compilers had provided us with a rationale for what they did. Lacking that, one has to do one's own detective work.

Roughly, it would appear that the selection has been based on a "harmony" of the gospels. Parallel passages, therefore, once used, are not repeated when a similar incident occurs in another evangelist (except for central incidents like the Baptism of Jesus, the Temptations in the Desert and the Transfiguration). This method provides a fairly large coverage of "Gospel Stories," but one is somewhat alarmed at what it does to the acknowledged fact that an evangelist uses each incident in his own special way, and gives it a nuance which expresses his particular theological insight.

Thus, at first, it seems that, by and large, the Gospel of Mark has been used as a basic text, being used almost in its entirety. Indeed, Mark Chapters 1 - 6 are used almost fully, over a period of sixteen weeks. The most characeristic part of Luke's gospel, the Journey Narrative, Chapters 9:51 – 19:27, is used, in bits, over nineteen Sundays. Matthew's five "sermons" account for twenty Sundays: The Sermon on the Mount, Chapters 5 – 7, the apostolic discourse, Chapter 10, the Parables, Chapter 13 (and also three parables Chapter 21:28 to Chapter 22), the Discourse on the Church, Chapter 18, and the Eschatological Discourse, Chapters 24 to 25.

(One notices a marked squeamishness about demons. The exorcism stories are omitted in all three years: Gerasene Demoniac, Mark 5:1-20, Epileptic Demoniac, Mark 9:14-29, and Luke 11:14-16, The Return of the Unclean Spirits.)

All things considered it does not seem to be too bad. Looking more closely however, one finds, for example, that Mark's finest piece of writing, what has been called "The Bread Section," Chapter 6:30 – 8:26, has been omitted, except for three mutilated scraps.

The same disillusionment faces us when we turn to Luke's Journey Narrative. Jerusalem has a central importance, as the place where God reveals himself, and the journey to Jerusalem is well-known as Luke's special literary device. As Conzelman put it: "For Luke, geography is theology." Luke frames his Journey Narrative between the second and third prophecies of the Passion, both of which are omitted. Stranger still, is that that most important scene in Luke's thought, Jesus's lament over Jerusalem (19:41-44), is also totally omitted. Counting the pericopes as subtitled in the *Jerusalem Bible*, the lectionary uses forty-five pericopes of Luke but omits another forty-four (excluding the Passion and Resurrection sections).

At every turn one is confronted with incongruities. On the second Sunday after Easter in Years 1 and 2, the gospel is taken from Luke Chapter 24. But in Year 3, when normally Luke's gospel is read, the reading for that Sunday is taken from John Chapter 21. The Emmaus story in Luke Chapter 24 is intimately connected with Luke's theological outlook that Jesus is rejected not just because he claims to be Messiah (as in Mark) but precisely because he presents himself as a Messiah who must suffer, like the anawim of the Old Testament. For Luke, the Resurrection is the fulfilment of the verse in the Magnificat: He lifts up the lowly – the anawim. Jesus who is raised from the dead is the perfect representative of the anawim.

Obviously, with Matthew, the compilers have opted to give us a fair representation of the Five Discourses. But this really brings us up against the fundamental inadequacy in the approach to all three gospels. Of course, the Sermon on the Mount, Matthew Chapters 5 – 7, is important; but in the scheme of St. Matthew's structure, the sermon does not make sense without the narrative section, which is totally omitted from the Sunday readings. As even the simplest popular introduction to Matthew recognises, this gospel is composed of five "books," each subdivided into a narrative section and a discourse. It does not make sense if the narrative section is consistently eliminated.

Nor is it enough to say that the material in Matthew 8 has been used in Year 2, Mark 1-2. Matthew uses the incidents to make a very different point. This is most easily seen if one compares the two verses telling of the Cure of Peter's mother-in-law as given in Matthew 8:14-15, and the parallel sections of Mark and Luke. No two details are the same in each of the three accounts, simply because each is using the incident to make a statement about his own special theological outlook about Jesus.

It really will not do, after so many years of scripture scholarship, when we have been made aware of the different "theologies" and "Christologies" in the bible, that the official lectionary should condemn us to return to something little better than a "stories from the bible" approach to scripture. The lectionary is still in continuity with that impoverished approach to scripture which regards the bible as a quarry, or museum collection, of "proof-texts" for some dogmatic or moral point of Church teaching.

Nor are these the quibbles of a pendant. The various theologies of the writers of the New Testament are, in their turn, the bases for the spirituality that derives from each of them; and that in turn greatly influences the practical moral response of the Christian.

In Year 3, we should be absorbing the spiritual insight of St. Luke, with its many strands; especially its embodiment of the Old Testament heritage of the anawim. A feeling for the spirituality of Luke is a far more urgent need for the average Christian today than explicit theological information and dogmatic statements. This is not to deny the great importance of theological statements, but it must also be recognised that even theological statements are themselves the distillation of a community's spirituality, in other words, the way it experiences spiritual reality, its awareness of the presence of God. It is not necessarily the technocrat or the economist, even the Christian economist, who will, in the end, solve the problems of poverty or injustice. It is men and women, whether literate or illiterate, it hardly matters, who have caught St. Luke's spirit of the anawim. They therefore know from the inside what Christian poverty and mercy and love really are, and what these demand.

It is strange that the Church still seems to operate on the socratic principle that knowledge is virtue: all we need to do is to educate people, make them literate. What men and women need is a spirituality. And that, precisely, is what the four gospels, each in its separate way, are all about. Yet, try as I may, I cannot see how, from the selections given for the Sunday readings, this can be done in regard to any one of the gospels.

Furthermore, the process is thoroughly confused by the fact that Lent and Easter intervene after the first six or seven weeks of the year, so that the normal progression, which should lead to the last chapters of the gospel, is dislocated.

Mark's gospel is frequently described as being "A Passion Narrative with Introduction." Since Lent begins around the seventh week of the year, we are given the Passion Narrative after Chapter 2. For the rest of the year we read the "introduction," which fizzles out with a meagre six verses from Chapter 13.

Perhaps this might simply imply that the reading of a particular gospel should stretch from after Trinity Sunday, through Advent, with its eschatological significance, and lead up to the Passion Narrative in Lent and Easter. There is nothing to be gained from counting the Sundays of the year from 1st January. Perhaps the old calendar, which numbered the Sundays after Pentecost or Trinity, would have been much more useful as a basis. (It is not accurate to regard Advent as a preparation for Christmas. Advent is the anticipation of the Second Coming.) Perhaps it would be best to think of the liturgical year as beginning after Pentecost of the previous year. Or, more precisely, does this fettish about assigning a beginning and an end to the liturgical year run altogether counter to the reality, which St. John so forcefully presents, of a continuing spiral.

A major cause of the difficulty with the lectionary is the brevity of the passages chosen, especially of the first and second readings on a Sunday. By a curious paradox, it is much more difficult to absorb a short passage which is out of its context, than to take in a much longer complete section. Why, for example, were the compilers so chicken-hearted in giving only three verses from Ezechiel's vision of the dry bones, Chapter 36 (fifth Sunday of Lent, Year 1)? The full passage is utterly enthralling to any congregation, and it is self-explanatory: but the snippet given in the Sunday lectionary comes across as only "another of those weak exhortations, couched in a complicated metaphor, which turn up week after week."

One is constantly struck by the failure of nerve, on the part of the compilers of the lectionary, to accept that scripture can communicate its message if it is given a chance. One senses that the compilers suspected that brevity is an antidote for boredom.

If a particular audience cannot take it the Directory of Children's Masses tells us what to do – omit it. But do not from the beginning make it doomed to be unintelligible by being presented out of context, and in a hopelessly truncated form. It is no solution to boredom just to shorten the boredom. In actual fact, the full passage on the dry bones takes two minutes thirty seconds to read aloud, quite effectively. The bit provided in the lectionary is a tedious thirty seconds; tedious because it is just enigmatic. Professor George Harrison makes the point that it is completely impossible for anyone, even a trained actor, effectively to proclaim a passage of scripture consisting of only fifty to one hundred words, as is the average Sunday reading. Even a trained actor cannot capture an audience and then convey a message, if that is his total exposure to them.

Even without major changes, it is possible, especially for weekday readings, to extend the passage assigned for that day. Most people who come to weekday Mass are quite ready for more than a tiny reading. For example, there is no reason why, on the three days assigned for reading the Letter to Titus, the three brief chapters of the epistle cannot be read in full. Read thus, as a unit, it makes more sense; otherwise, we get little more than three exhortatory paragraphs, which are unrelated to real people and real situations.

By and large, the number of weeks allotted for reading the epistles on weekdays makes it possible to do this quite easily. But, alas, many important parts of the Old Testament get a very raw deal. The charming but not very important Book of Tobit gets a week; but Proverbs, Ecclesiastes and Joshua get only three days each. Apart from three brief passages in Lent, Deuteronomy gets four days; thereby the whole basis of Deuteronomic History is omitted. The same becomes obvious in the readings from Samuel and Kings, where only the bits with human interest, in the journalistic sense, get a look in. The theological structure of the Books of Samuel and Kings – infidelity, punishment, repentance, deliverance – just does not appear.

Acts of the Apostle is read each year during the seven weeks of Easter. One might question whether it needs to be used every year, considering the vast omissions of other books. But more puzzling is the fact that Chapters 1 to 18 are spread over six weeks, and the last ten chapters get six days; and even at that, Paul's farewell at Ephesus is spread over two days – an outstanding instance of the proverbial "two bites at a cherry."

Despite the criticisms, let us add immediately that the outstanding value of the lectionary is that it presents us with a practical programme by which, over a two or three year period, we read through the whole of the New Testament and large parts of the Old Testament.

The thorough reading of one gospel every year, or of various other books of the New Testament or Old Testament on week days is the best programme for adult education that the Church has provided for centuries. Since the interim lectionary was introduced in 1966, we have read through most of the books of the bible six times at weekday Mass. The four gospels have been read four times each at Sunday Mass.

One might feel at first that it is hard to explain how people could read through such a limited collection of books six times in twelve years and still be so unfamiliar with the contents, or with the distinctiveness of each particular book. Once more, we must remember that liturgy forms us by a slower process. Valuable though such information may be, a clear analytical knowledge of a gospel is not our primary objective. But if scripture itself is given a chance, it will form us over the years with the insights that come from familiarity and love. It is in this sense that St. Jerome says "Ignorance of scripture is ignorance of Christ." That ignorance cannot be cured by a rapid reading of commentaries. Prolonged familiarity alone forms the "mind of Christ" in us.

In the programme of weekday reading, the lectionary assigns various books of the bible for reading each week. Retaining this as a basic plan, it is possible to enlarge the passage given for any particular day so that in the daily readings particular books are read in full. This can be easily achieved with almost all the books of the New Testament. The average weekday congregation readily appreciates a slightly lengthened reading which links up with the readings of previous days.

This familiarity with scripture leads to the key insight regarding scripture in the Christian life. Each writer in the bible has his own special theological outlook and spirituality. Each book of scripture deals with different spiritual crises in the life of the People of God and of the early Christian communities. Every crises and difficulty experienced by Christians in their journey through life has, in fact, been dealt with at various places in these books. And somewhere over the three year cycle of the lectionary we will have been given an opportunity to reflect on it in the liturgy.

The normal way in which spiritual direction was given in the whole pre-Reformation tradition was simply through daily comments on the readings in the liturgy given by a bishop, or by an abbot in his monastery. It is still true that nearly all the spiritual direction we need is provided for us by the Church through the daily reading in the Mass. This is the Church's normal way of nourishing her children and guiding them. In this way we are given an understanding of the Christian map of life. It is a map of life which is, for each one of us, our journey through the desert into the promised land.

The Psalter

The Constitution on the Liturgy, and other decrees, have some very idealistic and promising remarks to make on the use of the Psalter. They suggest that by the use of the psalms in the Mass, Christians would again come to the point of being able to use some of the psalms as their daily prayer.

We have already dealt with the unsatisfactoriness of using brief spoken responses in reciting the psalms, the "response" being of its nature a text for a musical setting. It also becomes evident on examination that none of the psalms is used often enough to become familiar.

It turns out that of the whole one hundred and fifty psalms, only a handful are used more than five times in the whole three year cycle. In the Sunday and weekday cycles, Psalm 129, Out of the depths . . . is used a total of four times. Thus it is rather fanciful to expect that anyone could become so familiar with the psalm that it could become part of his ordinary prayers.

Psalm 116, "Praise the Lord . . ." which we knew from Benediction, is used a total of three times in the whole lectionary. The Good Shepherd Psalm, only seven times. Of the seven Penitential Psalms, which our parents or grandparents' generation would have known by heart, even if they did not know the word "psalm," three are totally omitted.

Psalm 42, which all of us know: "I will go to the altar of God . . ." is used once.

Psalm 41: "Like the deer that yearns for running streams . . ." is used three times.

Psalm 62, "O God, thou art my God . . ." which for the first one thousand years of Christianity was used every day as the morning prayer of every Christian, is used only twice in the lectionary.

COURSES FOR READERS

Surely one of the most difficult and delicate tasks in preparing the liturgy is first the choice of readers, and then their training. Since people still commonly think of the readings at Mass as not being very important, it is hard to convey, even to readers, that they have to read well, or not at all. Such a statement as this will probably arouse great indignation. To "read well" is easily assumed to imply that everyone is excluded who has not received training in elocution. Indeed, some basic ideas about how to speak in public are indispensable, but even that does not guarantee that someone will read well, or should be a reader at Mass. The point is perhaps best illustrated by an article published in *Doctrine and Life*, by Desmond Fennell, entitled *What I Miss in Sermons*. The gist of one particular response was: "What I miss in sermons is a man talking." It requires a particular skill to talk aloud, and not seem unnatural. A few people can do it very well without specific training; training in elocution seems to guarantee that other people will never again speak naturally. But the majority of us need training, and in this matter one can never be one's own judge.[2]

The only comment offered here in this regard is that it would be unnecessarily burdensome to impose a general course in speech training on everyone. Yet, at the same time, training and practice in reading scripture must extend over a long period, even for good readers. Not even the best of advice can be assimilated in a few sessions. One should never read scripture at Mass without having practised it, aloud, preferably in the presence of a helpful critic.

But more important than speech training, is formation of another kind. Reading well presumes that one understands the passage being read. This in turn demands that one understands the context from which the passage is taken. It is probably too much to expect that lay-people will normally be able to do this preparation on their own, and so it would seem desirable that all the readers for Masses on any particular Sunday should be given some

---

[2] An excellent handbook for readers is *Proclaiming the Word*, by G.B. Harrison and John McCabe, published by Pueblo Publishing Company, New York.

such background instruction together. Perhaps in this regard we need to revert to the type of regular formation programme used by groups like the Legion of Mary and other apostolic societies. In fact, in the early Church, the whole congregation came together three times a week to prepare the Sunday's readings. This explains how the Church Fathers could make so many obscure references to Old Testament passages when preaching to people who had been only recently converted.

Readers at least need some of this formation. Then in time they will come to see that they have a ministry of the Word to their own parish. They will become aware that their ministry does not end with the reading of ten lines from the lectionary on Sunday morning. In time, as they develop in their sense of responsibility to those to whom they read, they will recognise that there is a special charism, or gift from God, of proclaiming the Word of God.

What we need most in training readers is a time when they can reflect on scripture, and when they can achieve that familiarity with scripture which enables them to speak it as something which they have found to be precious and formative. As a result, the reader can say, in his whole presentation: This is important to me; this is the Word of the Lord.

With these remarks we can set about the task of implementing that most basic of all the reforms introduced by the Liturgical Constitution, where it says that the Mass consists of two parts: The liturgy of the Word and the liturgy of the Eucharist. Our task is to enable others to participate in the liturgy of the Word so that they will know it as an experience of Christ's presence, by whom they are healed and in whom they live.

9 THE LITURGY OF
THE EUCHARIST

THE TREATMENT of the liturgy of the Eucharist falls into three distinct areas.

1. Some comments on the Eucharistic liturgy as it is now normally experienced. This leads us to ask: how successful is the present liturgy as ritual; what are its inadequacies; and how easily can they be corrected?
2. An explanation of the theology of the Eucharist, or the theory underlying the ritual.
3. A summary analysis of the structure and content of the Eucharistic prayers.

These three areas are, however, so closely interlocked that they must first be dealt with together before any attempt at a detailed analysis of each. It is a curious flaw in our approach to liturgy that it is always presumed that one first has to work out an elaborate theory or theology of the sacrament, and then at a subsequent stage, invent a ritual in which to express this theory.

Anthropologists are amazed that anyone would have attempted to reform the liturgy by committee. In the whole history of mankind, they say, ritual has never been drawn up by committees. One does not start with an explicit theory that is to be portrayed or taught, and then invent ritual, like visual aids for a classroom. Rather, the community wants to express the core of its understanding of life, and celebrate it, and pass it on; and they do this in rituals which are produced, refined and enriched over centuries of use. The business of reducing this life-understanding to a clearly expressed philosophical system, or a series of theological dogmas or doctrines, is a much later step in the process. In fact, it is something in which the non-expert, the non-theologian, usually is not involved.

Yet the community's rituals, and for the Catholic that means our liturgy, are the most important way in which its belief is expressed. The Latin adage was "lex orandi, lex credendi," which means that the way people pray is the best indicator of what they believe. Our liturgy is the most accurate expression of what, in Catholic theology, is called the "sensus fidelium," the sure instinct by which the Holy Spirit guides the body of the faithful, keeping them always in tune with Christ's word. More than anything else, it is the liturgy that forms in us "the mind of Christ."

In turn, the liturgy is also one of the primary sources of theological reflection on the meaning of any sacrament. That means that if one wants to know what baptism means, the first source to consult is not a catechism, or a book of theology, but the rite of Baptism. Better still, one should attend a baptism and experience what happens there. It is always astounding how the Christian community instinctively retains the balance of the theological statement made in any particular sacrament, even at times when secondary ritual elements are being given undue importance.

A good example of this instinct in operation is seen in the history of the Canon of the Mass. For centuries the Canon of the Mass was sung aloud. Then, other music developed which tended to swamp the Eucharist Prayer. Gradually, but with utmost accuracy, the Eucharistic Prayer was given new and even greater prominence, by being recited in an awe-inspiring silence. So, in time, silence became an even more powerful symbol than song. In this way the instinct for high-lighting what is important re-asserted itself.

The liturgical reforms of Vatican II recognised quite accurately that the Eucharistic Prayer is itself the supreme proclamation of the gospel message, Christ has died, Christ is risen, and therefore, it ought again to be proclaimed aloud, in the language people know. Other singing and ritual should, therefore, again be put in a subsidiary role. We are now, once more, trying consciously to achieve a balance between all these elements. No culture or ritual has even before had to attempt such a task. It is as though a decision were made that, in future, English kings and queens would be inaugurated in the manner of American presidents at a mass gathering in Trafalgar Square, with everyone dressed in jeans. The task presented to the committees who were to draw up the new liturgy was really as radical as that, really as unprecedented as that. How could you crown a king in Trafalgar Square, forgetting all the one thousand years of ceremonial attached to the present coronation rite? How would you invent new and adequate ritual, and yet retain all the basic meaning?

VIEWING THE EUCHARIST LITURGY

I shall therefore start my comments on the reformed liturgy of the Eucharist by making a statement which, I suppose, most people would regard as being outrageously unrealistic. It is now quite normal for us to be able to use unleavened bread, which looks more like bread, tastes like bread, and must be eaten like bread and which is broken from one loaf. It is quite normal, on most occasions when we wish, that everyone may receive communion from the chalice. Therefore, I honestly think that the basic ritual elements in the liturgy of the Eucharist are, to my mind, completely satisfactory. I cannot think of any further improvements that I should want to make. Especially is this true when you add the fact that it is also normal to have special ministers of communion, so that the communion can be distributed to each individual slowly and prayerfully.

The sacred elements of bread and wine, placed solemnly on the altar at the Preparation of the Gifts, shown to the people after the words of Institution, raised up in the act of offering at the great doxology, "through Him, with Him, in Him," divided at the breaking of the bread, at the Agnus Dei, and then offered to each individual at the communion, these sacred signs truly dominate the whole liturgy of the Eucharist. They over-arch it, and create a unity which is most powerful. All that is needed now is that we learn to give them our attention. We must learn to look at the bread and wine, as they stand there, throughout the whole rite, always visible.

Of course, there are some flaws in the new liturgy of the Eucharist, but these are mostly due to the texts. The texts give the impression of a series of poorly connected devotional exercises and prayers, which do not hang together very well. As a result, no matter how well the Eucharist prayers are spoken, the attention of the congregation obviously strays quite a lot. Their attention is recaptured by the congregation's recited or sung parts: Holy, Holy, Eucharistic acclamation, Great Amen, and later, the Our Father, and by the sign of peace. Yet, I must re-affirm my conviction that the four places in the Mass at which the bread and wine are pointed to and emphasised, create the true unity, which is realised for each individual personally at its fullest as he looks at the sacred host lying in his or her own hand. The silence and awe of that moment is the most powerful ritual I have ever experienced, no matter how many people there are to whom I have to give communion.

Some years ago, it was not at all obvious that the Mass was a meal of bread and wine. In the old Latin rite, the bread was seen only for the moment when it was held above the priest's head at the elevation; the wine was not seen at all. In fact, anyone far from the altar could not see anything. The position is now completely reversed. The dominance given to the symbols of the bread and wine create the real unity; and from this point of view, this establishes the satisfactoriness of the new rite.

Still, it would be unrealistic not to acknowledge that even a short passage like the "Holy, Holy," is defective in some way. People obviously find that their attention wanders, even when they are singing or saying the Sanctus. I suspect that what happens is that the second part, "Blessed is he," is recited on the tail-end of a breath. In a Gregorian setting of the Sanctus, or any polyphonic setting, the second part, "Blessed is he," is a new start, with a new assertion of importance. In Gregorian chant, with its alternations between cantors and choir, the Sanctus was a form of litany. In our present usage – where all say or sing the whole text, the second half never catches the importance of this new statement and attention dribbles away. The last section of this chapter will return to a discussion of the texts of the Eucharistic prayers.

THE THEOLOGY OF THE EUCHARIST

First however, we need to examine some of the elements of our Eucharistic theology. We need to uncover the theory about the Eucharist with which we approach the liturgy. Inaccurate theory always leads to a misinterpretation of even the most perfect symbols. If one has a theory (or an assumption) that everyone who wears a three-piece suit is a gentleman, and his word can always be trusted, one is in for some bad shocks in life. Every con-man in the country knows that half the population actually believes that proposition. If he has the right status symbols, that is, if he has the right ritual; collar-and-tie, car, office in town, home in the right suburb, no-one will question his integrity, and they will trust him with all their worldly possessions.

What then do we do with the Eucharistic symbols; what sort of theory have we got at the back of our minds which we apply to these symbols? How do we interpret them? Bad theory can misinterpret and distort even perfect symbols.

The encyclopedia, *Sacramentum Mundi*, (Vol. II pp. 274-276) gives a brief history of the theological theories proposed over the centuries to help explain the Eucharist. In particular, it speaks of the theory of immolation or destruction, commonly known as the Immolation Theory. The Immolation Theory was, in fact, the theory about the Eucharist which most of us were given in school. The article describes how this theory developed in the 17th century, about fifty years after the Reformation. At the time of the Reformation, Catholic theologians retained strongly the sense that the Eucharist is a sacrament, a symbol, a ritual of a sacrifice. In St. Thomas's phrase: the Eucharist is a sacrament of the sacrifice of Calvary. It is a symbol, sacred sign, which expresses Christ's sacrifice.

A half century later, after the Reformation crisis itself, something occurred which happens regularly in history: Catholic theologians began to take their opponents' definition as the starting point for their own discussions and began trying to explain the Mass in terms of the Protestant definition of sacrifice. They started from the Protestant view, that sacrifice necessarily involved the destruction of a victim. Therefore, they asserted, if the Mass is a sacrifice, something physically destructive must happen to Jesus.

The Immolationist theories then, were worked out on this basically Protestant presupposition. These 17th century theologians tried to defend the Mass as a sacrifice in terms of this quite unacceptable definition of sacrifice.

"During the early controversies with the Reformers, in the pre-Tridentine period, the essentially sacramental characters of the Eucharist had still been acknowledged on the Catholic side, but now it was lost sight of. Catholic defenders of the sacrificial character of Mass thus took their stand on the chosen ground of the Reformers – the purely natural conception according to which sacrifice necessarily means expiation in blood (*offerri* = *mori*).

"Post-Tridentine theologians were forced to suppose that at Mass something natural is done *to* Christ mysteriously present under the appearances of bread and wine. This mistaken idea was most forcefully expressed in what are known as the theories of destruction, which asserted that in some manner or other Christ sacramentally present underwent a destruction, or at least a transformation (*immutatio, immolatio*). Some (like Lessius [d.1623], realising how difficult it is to entertain the idea that a physical change takes place in Christ who is now glorified, put forward the modified view that the words of consecration merely aimed at separating the body and blood of Christ and so at his death, while the actual effect did not follow, on account of his impassible state. Others (like J. de Lugo [d.1660] and J. Franzelin [d.1886] supposed the element of sacrifice to consist in the state of humiliation brought about by the consecration, where Christ now proffers himself as food to men.

"Modern theologians are reverting to an essentially sacramental idea of the sacrifice of the Mass, such as the great Fathers and the Schoolmen basically propounded. When the categories of sacramental being are applied consistently to the eucharistic sacrifice, we realise that Mass is "the sacrament of the sacrifice of the cross," in which Christ's redemption becomes present through the ministry of the priest in a memorial which is an image of the reality, without any need of a special and literal act of sacrifice. If the symbolic character of the sacrifice of the Mass is stressed, its strict identity with the sacrifice of the cross will be satisfactorily preserved; furthermore, we can then fully recognise the symbolic character of the liturgical rite, which explains why Mass takes the form of a meal; and finally, it then becomes possible for the Church and the faithful to be organically drawn into the sacramental representation of Christ's sacrifice, for the Church inwardly and actively associates itself with the sacrifice of Christ by positing the sacramental sign that proclaims its assent to the Lord's sacrifice and its own sacrificial dispositions."

(Sacramentum Mundi)

The commonest version of the Immolation Theory is what most of us probably received in school: the death of Christ is expressed in the Mass by the separate consecrations; the separate consecrations brought about the separation of the body and the blood, and therefore they symbolise and make real the death of Christ; somehow the death of Jesus was mimed.[1]

There were other related theories, such as, that Our Lord was in a state of humiliation in the Eucharist, the humiliation of making himself to be a piece of bread for us, and that his sacrifice consists in this humiliation. This was the theory of Franzelin, who died in 1886. Out of that theory derived the 19th century piety to Jesus as "The Sweet Prisoner of the Tabernacle."

Each of these theories tries to establish that the Mass is a sacrifice because, somehow, in it, Our Lord is subjected to death or humiliation.

One must hasten to say that neither of these explanations is heretical. But they are not in line with the long history of Catholic theology of the Mass, and they lead to a limited understanding. They are based on an idea of the Mass as a miming of Our Lord's Passion, rather than as a sacrament, a sacred sign, part of ritual. There is no question but that they have supported the devotion of Catholics for generations, and elements of them can still be of great value in enriching our own devotion. They did put us in tune with what was happening at Mass, just as the Rosary led generations of Catholics to a fruitful sharing in the Eucharist.

---

[1] At this point it might be well to remember that crucifixion was in fact a "bloodless" form of execution. It was a form of hanging. In itself it did not involve shedding blood, as does, for example, beheading.

St. John and St. Paul use the words *Blood,* or *Blood of Christ*, not primarily to refer to the physical blood of Our Lord, but as a verbal shorthand, to express their fundamental theology that Jesus was establishing the New Covenant. In his life and death, in his "going to the Father" he supersedes and fulfils all that the offering of the Paschal Lamb had been in the Old Testament. St. John's account of the Passion tells nothing of the agony and brutality suffered by Jesus, as described in the Synoptic Gospels. Every detail of John's account is explicitly demonstrating that Jesus is the true Paschal Lamb.

However, these theories are not adequate in helping us to understand the theological outlook of the Constitution on the Liturgy. And if one is not aware that these theories arise from a different definition of sacrifice, one is always left in a state of puzzlement, as one tries to reconcile various paragraphs of the Constitution on the Liturgy with the ideas about the sacraments stored at the back of one's head since school days. We are unaware that, basically, these two approaches are quite irreconcilable.

The pre-Reformation understanding of the Eucharist, based on the essential sacramental character of the Eucharist, did not re-appear in Catholic writing until the publication of Abbot Vonier's book *The Key to the Doctrine of the Eucharist*, in 1924.[2] It was in this book that Vonier retrieved St. Thomas's basic theory of the meaning of sacrament, and of the Eucharist as "a sacrament of the sacrifice of Calvary." This rediscovery of sacramental theology, in the sense of sacred signs, in turn gave the liturgical reforms the momentum which set them in the right direction. Once more we had a theology of the Eucharist which understood ritual.

Part of our present task is to acquire an understanding of this theological outlook, which is, in fact, the great traditional understanding of the Eucharist as a sacrament.[3]

Another distinction, which will be remembered from school days, is that between *sacrament* and *sacrifice*. It used to be said that the Consecration was the sacrifice, and that Holy Communion was the sacrament. This also is quite an inappropriate distinction. One has to say that the

[2]It is interesting to notice that in the bibliography at the end of the article in *Sacramentum Mundi, The Key to the Doctrine of the Eucharist* is given with its 1952 republication date, but if we remember that it was originally published in English in 1924, it becomes the earliest published book in that whole bibliography.

[3]Two other books could be recommended which are shorter and simplier than Vonier: Roguet: *Sacraments, Acts of Christ* and McCabe: *New Creation*. In time, however, one should take the trouble to read Vonier thoroughly. Then one could further recommend Schillebeeckx: *Christ the Sacrament*.

Consecration is both sacrament and sacrifice, and that communion is both sacrament and sacrifice. Or rather, that the whole Eucharistic liturgy is the sacrament of the sacrifice of Christ. The Mass is a sacrament of the sacrifice of Calvary.

The Scriptural Notion of Sacrifice

At this stage we obviously need to clarify the idea of sacrifice, to get away from the Reformation assumption that "sacrifice equals death or destruction." In this regard, it is most helpful to examine the idea of sacrifice in scripture. There are many kinds of sacrifice described in the bible, and it is significant that most of them do not refer to death or pain. The biblical notion of sacrifice really has nothing to do with pain. Sacrifice is about trying to find something that will adequately express one's love for someone, most particularly, one's love for God. Something that will adequately express our covenant relationship with the Lord. It is like trying to find a suitable Christmas present, something that would adequately express one's love for this person. The fact that one is $20 the poorer, really does not enter one's thoughts.

But the English word "sacrifice" has come to refer particularly to the inconvenience one puts up with for the sake of someone else. Perhaps it is, as Napolean observed, the shop-keeper mentality of the English-speaking world that has made us concentrate on the cost. In the bible, the word sacrifice means that one does something which expresses the intensity of one's love. There is no thought of its cost, in terms of money or of personal inconvenience. It surely never even crossed Mary's thoughts that the pot of ointment could have been sold for three hundred denarii, and the money put to useful purposes. Real love always has some element of what St. Thomas calls the virtue of magnificence, the virtue that is thoughtless of expense, in its desire to express its love adequately.

In Jewish practice, the various types of sacrifice express different aspects of one's dedication to God. There were special times, days or weeks, which were set aside for God – time you spent with him, because you loved him. In this way the Sabbath day was, is the best sense of the word, a sacrifice. Hair-sacrifice is another of the unlikely ways of making sacrifice. The best known example of this was Samson, who was a Nazarite. In this particular case one vowed oneself to God for a specific time, and during that period one's hair remained uncut. At the end of the period, the hair was shorn off, and the hair was then offered in sacrifice, as it were, handing over one's bodily beauty to God. But the main kinds of sacrifice were those involving blood and food.

A preliminary thought to the idea of blood sacrifice was that one gave God a gift of something which was part of the family, for example, a pet lamb, to express one's closeness to God. It was not unlike the Polynesian custom of children being reared in the family of an uncle or by a grandparent, so that parts of one's own family were living at the centre of other parts of the family or tribe. In this way, the pet lamb was to be given to God, in order to express how you wanted to live within the circle of his life. It is not death you offer to God, but life. Sacrifice is about expressing your sense of lovingly being-with-God.

It was at this point that the Jews used the symbol of blood, to express this giving of one's living love to God, this being in the living presence of God, this living in him. For the Jews, blood was the living thing, the moving thing, in a living organism. (The killing of the lamb was quite secondary, and it was not performed by the priests, but by special temple attendants.) The blood of the lamb was drained and then the blood was brought to the priest. What had been done was that somehow in this chalice or vessel of blood, the life of this little animal had been caught. Not only this; the vessel of blood seemed to capture and express the whole life of this family, almost as a perfume captures that most intangible thing, the fragrance of a flower. So in this way, the blood was thought of as having captured this intangible thing – life. And it was the living blood, the blood that symbolised the living life of this family, that was brought to the Lord.

The priest then took the blood and poured in on the altar. The altar was the place consecrated to God, a place where, in the past, God had revealed himself to the patriarchs. God's presence had been experienced there, as at the rock of the temple, where by tradition, Abraham had received his revelation. The priest poured the blood on the altar, like a child throwing an armful of wild flowers into its mothers's lap.

But once the blood had touched the altar is was seen as having come in contact with God. It was seen now, not as just a symbol of life given to God, but as being charged with God's life. Therfore, after this (as is described in the sacrifice for the cleansing of a leper: Lev. 14), the priest took some of the blood from the altar and sprinkled it over the people, or touched the tip of the ear, the tip of the thumb and the tip of the toe of the person to be consecrated. The symbolism of blood sacrifice is the symbolism of blood flowing, as it does in the human body from left hand through to the right hand, keeping the body alive as one organism. So too, blood-sacrifice for the Jews might be expressed in modern terms by saying that it symbolised organic unity of life with God – our life flowing out into God and God's life flowing back into us. We are made the one living body of God.

Food sacrifice involved an exactly parallel way of thinking. Even in our own culture, to invite someone home for a meal is not usually a question of supplementing his diet. What one is doing is inviting another to be part of one's family life for this little time. So, food sacrifice, the setting aside of part of one's food for the Lord, followed a similar pattern to that of blood-sacrifice. The food was brought to the altar, as a way of inviting God to be part of one's family life. Once again, when the priest put it on the altar, God, as it were, reverses the invitation, and invites us home to dinner with him instead. The food that has touched the altar is seen as changed. It has come into contact with God – almost like needles touching a magnet, each being magnetised; it is the food of God's table, it is no longer our food, but God's food. The food was then taken by the priest and shared with those who had first brought it. And the symbolism in this case is that of family unity of life with God; God sharing his love, sharing his life with us; God renewing the covenant: "you will be my people, and I will be your God, and I, to whom the whole world belongs, will single you out to be my very own."

Sacrifice and covenant are two inter-related ideas, which have no meaning without each other. Sacrifice is the way in which the love-covenant between God and man is begun, and then constantly renewed. It has essentially very little to do with pain, except that loving fidelity to God will inevitably put us at loggerheads with the world. God's children will always suffer because of that fidelity. But the suffering is quite secondary.

Closely related to the idea of sacrifice-covenant, is the word *symbolum*, in its earliest usage. The ancient way of making a contract was to take a coin, and snap it in two; each party in the contract then kept half of the coin. This broken coin was called a symbolum. At any time one person could present his half-coin to the other, either to remind him of their mutual agreement, or to demand its fulfilment. It was like a finger print guaranteeing one's authenticity and identity. The fact that the two halves fitted together was the guarantee, the signature, that this was really the person with whom the contract had been made. But more important than mere identification, the symbolum reminded each of the conditions of their contract, and demanded its fulfilment. An example of this procedure is described in the Book of Tobit, Ch. 3.

Sacrifice was of the same nature. It was as though God put into our hands an IOU, by which we could remind him of his covenant and his promise, and demand their fulfilment.

The commonest simile God uses in the bible for his covenant with his people is the marriage covenant between husband and wife. The ordinary details of family life are the best means of illustrating that covenant between God and his people. Any ordinary couple, prior to their marriage, will have given each other various gifts, boxes of chocolates, or an engagement ring, as tokens by which they promised that in the future they would give themselves totally. Those gifts were a symbolum, a token expressing the promise which eventually they fulfilled in their marriage itself.

Later on, at Christmas and wedding anniversaries, they still feel the need to give tokens, presents. The common experience of many families is that when the husband buys a present for his wife he will wrap it up and then get one of the children to give the present to its mother. What he is doing, instinctively, is that he is enabling the child to enter into, and to express, a love far beyond what it, as a child, is capable of understanding. The child becomes the vehicle by which the husband's love for his wife is conveyed; the mother's return love for her husband is likewise expressed through the child. The child is caught up in the sweep of the father's love for his wife, and in the mother's return gift of love.

This is very much what Our Lord had done for us in giving us the Eucharist. Like the child saying to his mother: "Daddy said to give you this," Jesus has given us the way of saying to the Father, as we bring the bread and wine, "Jesus said to give you this." He places in our hands the symbolum by which we are caught up in the sweep of the Son's love for the Father, which found its ultimate expression in his death, and the Father's return gift of resurrection, of life, to Jesus.

Anamnesis: Memoria

The technical word for the Canon of the Mass is the Greek word *anamnesis* – the memorial: Do this in memory of me. The word is similar to the word "amnesia" – loss of memory. In English, to turn a word into its negative one puts *un* before the first syllable of the word: like – *un*like; enlighten – *un*enlightened. In Greek one adds the syllable *an*. So the word amnesia, loss of memory, becomes *an*amnesia – an inability to forget, or to remember in a particularly powerful way. St. Paul refers to the Eucharist as the memorial, the anamnesis of the death of the Lord.

The Paschal Supper was for the Jews the annual memorial of their deliverance from Egypt. But this was not a mere calling to mind a past event, like flicking through an old photograph album. The paschal supper was an anamnesis, a reliving of the events of God's saving action in the past, by which all that he did for our ancestors in the past was now actually done for us. Those who celebrate the memorial share totally in that event of the past; and God's saving presence enfolds us now as truly as it sheltered and sanctified our ancestors in the past. The bible gives the account of how that presence was experienced in the past when God first made his covenant. What God creates first is a people and a covenant, and then a world, for the people to inhabit. As each succeeding generation celebrated the paschal supper that covenant and that promise became a reality for them.

The Mass as the anamnesis, as the memorial of the Last Supper, must now be recognised as being a memorial, not in the shallow sense in which we have Remembrance Day, nor even in the way that a crib is a memorial of Bethlehem. When St. Paul talks about the Eucharist as a memorial he means that the events of Calvary and the Resurrection are present here, and they produce here in us the very same effects as they had in the beginning. We are drawn into that event and we share in it – the event by which Jesus goes to the Father and receives from the Father the glory of his Sonship.

Maori culture too, has close points of contact with the Jewish notion of a memorial, as when at the meeting house, they first address the dead. By this, they remember the dead, and also keep us aware that their deeds live on, that we stand on the shoulders of the living-dead. The Maori Battalion, returning to Monte Casino recently, caught something of the sense that history is part of the present. God who is timeless is present to all time. God's acts are not limited by human temporalness.

The Sacred Meal

St. Thomas' prayer for the feast of Corpus Christi sums up the doctrine of Eucharist perfectly:

O Sacrum convivium
In quo Christus sumitur
Recolitur memoria passionis eius
Mens impletur gratia
Et futurae gloriae nobis pignus datur.

O sacred banquet: this is no ordinary meal, but a special kind of ritual meal. We are in the area of ritual, in which Christ is received, consumed. The memorial of his passion is recalled – the anamnesis of the passion. The mind is filled with grace. The pledge of future glory is given to us. The Greek word for pledge is *ararbon* –token or a promise. It is like the sip of wine given by the waiter after opening the bottle, to taste it and enjoy it, and assure you that there is an endless supply of the same waiting for you if you want it. It is a foretaste. (There is no corresponding word in English.) The Eucharist is that kind of foretaste of future life, a foretaste of sharing in the life of Christ in God.

St. Thomas calls the Mass a banquet. It is not enough to say that the Mass is a meal. In every culture there are many different kinds of meals. In our society we have, for example, breakfast, lunch, tea, dinner; and each has quite different "rituals." Then there are such things as fish-and-chips, a picnic or a "cut-lunch," a quick cup of tea, a birthday party, Sunday dinner with the family, a wedding

breakfast. There are vast differences in the messages conveyed by any one of these meals. Each of these *says* something different.

The only meal that I can think of in Western culture
which is purely ritual is the drinking of a toast, like the
drinking of a toast at a wedding or an anniversary or a
funeral. A toast has no connection with diet or calories.
It is purely ritual. Unless one is willing to enter into the
area of ritual it is impossible to make sense of such a phrase
as "I ask you to charge your glasses and drink a toast to . . . ."
A milestone in the life of these people is being celebrated.
Someone among them is committing himself to these people
in a special way, or he has proved his commitment, in his
whole life which is now being recalled, or perhaps they are
drinking a toast to someone who, through twenty-five years
of fidelity in marriage or in some other vocation, has bound
himself to the community. Strange as it may seem, drinking
a toast is still directly connected with the ancient style of
making a covenant, or re-affirming with gratitude a covenant already made in the past.

The toast is the only kind of purely ritual eating and
drinking that we Europeans possess. It is the nearest
example of what is implied in the idea of a sacred banquet.
When we eat and drink this toast, in memory of the Lord's
death and resurrection, we are not only reminding ourselves
of our debt to the Lord, but we are also presenting before
the Father the symbolum, the covenant-sign, which Christ
has given us to remind the Father of his covenant promise.
That promise is fulfilled already in regard to Jesus, but as
yet it is still unfulfilled in regard to us. As we hold the host
in our hands and drink the cup we are saying to the Father:
"Remember Calvary." That is the statement implicit in
the words "This is the Blood of the Covenant." The statement is addressed to the Father; but also to us. Jesus was
not just addressing the apostles when he used the priestly
words from the Old Testament: "This is the Blood of the
Covenant that Yahweh has made with His people." The

words of Institution in the Mass, like the whole of the Eucharistic prayer, are directed and addressed primarily to the Father. We are addressing the Father, calling on him to remember the covenant he made. We are demanding that he fulfil his promise to give us new life in Christ, his Son, who died and rose from the dead.

ANALYSIS OF EUCHARISTIC PRAYERS

The last area to be dealt with is the analysis of the Eucharistic prayers themselves. The following division shows how one authority, E.J. Lengkling, categories the various parts which make up a Eucharistic prayer:

A. Those parts that are indispensably constitutive:
   Praise and thanksgiving for the mystery of salvation,
   The Institution narrative,
   The anamnesis, or remembrance of the Paschal mystery,
   A doxology.

B. Those elements that form an integral part of the Prayer without being indispensable:
   Mention of the sacrificial character,
   The epiclesis, or invocation of the Holy Spirit,
   Communion with the local church and the Church universal;

C. Those elements that should not be omitted in principle, but whose presence may be limited:
   The Sanctus,
   Communion with the heavenly liturgy,
   The communion of saints,
   The memento of the living and the dead;

D. Those elements that may be in the Prayer, and are even desirable:
   Praise and thanksgiving for the work of creation,
   A prayer for the acceptance of the sacrifice,
   The mention of present concerns,
   The responses of the community.

It is a worthwhile exercise to take each of the nine prayers which are now available for general use, and place each paragraph, and each sentence in its appropriate category.

Another simple manner of analysing the Eucharistic prayer is to see that in it *someone* is speaking to *someone* about *something*. Try to identify each of these: the speaker, the listener and what is being spoken of. For example, take the words of Institution: "This is my Body." At first sight it seems obvious that in these words Jesus is speaking to us, the congregation. Many priests in fact break the bread at this point, or even if they do not break the bread, they visually pass it around, with a gesture of offering it to the congregation. Obviously they have not read the whole sentence. The whole sentence is addressed to the Father throughout, spoken by the priest, in the name of the Church. The words of Institution are in reported speech, "in inverted commas." The sense is basically "Father, Jesus told us to give you this." The Eucharistic prayer is addressed to the Father throughout. It is not addressed to the congregation; at most we "overhear" what is said. In speaking to the Father, the priest quotes the words of Jesus at the Last Supper.

It is easier to catch this sense if we remember again that in an Old Testament covenant-sacrifice, the Jewish priest said the words "This is the blood of the covenant" as he poured the blood on the altar, and sprinkled it over the people. Again, in the Old Testament context, the priest was primarily addressing Yahweh, and then, in Yahweh's name, proclaiming to the people the covenant which God was making with them.

An impoverished idea of Christian priesthood has reduced the sacrament of Holy Orders to a conferring of the power to say the words of Consecration by which transubstantiation is achieved. This notion of Holy Orders bears a strong family likeness to the idea of the Mass described by Maisie Ward as "a machine for making Holy Communion." The priest's role in this strange, but common, theory of the Eucharist is that he is momentarily taken over by Jesus, who performs "the miracle of transubstan-tiation." In correcting this idea we must strongly assert that the Eucharist is not a miracle; it is a sacrament. The Eucharist or any sacrament, is a totally different category of reality from a miracle. Priesthood is not a magical power conferred on an individual, which is, from here on, his private possession, so that he could, from sheer spite, walk into a bakery and "say the words." If sacraments are liturgy, and therefore ritual, they exist only when all the other requirements for valid ritual are present. If the priest has not even a minimal intention of being involved in the rite, or ritual by which the covenant between God and his people is renewed, nothing happens. If the primary reality of the covenant-sacrifice is not being celebrated, then most certainly, the secondary reality of transubstantiation is not present.

So, in the Eucharistic prayer, the priest is not miming what Jesus did and said. Neither is he addressing the congre-gation. Rather, it is that he, the priest, and the congregation together, express their united confidence as they stand in the presence of the Father, because Jesus told us to "take and eat this all of you."

At this point we could well link up with the previous remarks on *memorial*. We need to ask the question: When Jesus said "Do this in memory of me" who is to do the remembering?

One prominent scholar replies that it is the Father who does the remembering. When Jesus said "Do this in memory of me" he was not just saying to the disciples: "keep me in mind occasionally." Rather, it is like the words of the thief on the cross: "Jesus, remember me when you come into your kingdom" or the words of Psalm 24: "Remember not the sins of my youth, Lord, in your love, remember me."

The whole Eucharistic prayer is addressed to the Father, and in it we call on the Father to remember his promise. This is brought out well at various points in the new Eu-charistic prayers which use repeated phrases like "Father, remember your church ... Father remember those who have gone before us in the light of faith." We ask the Father to remember his covenant-promise, spoken to us through the Lord Jesus: "As the Father has life, and I live by the Father, so he who eats me will live in me." The Father has already fulfilled his promise by raising up Jesus, but his promise is not yet completely fulfilled in our regard. "Remember the dead – you promised to raise them up; now, in the name of Jesus, fulfil your promise."

An unfortunate confusion arises from the use of the words "Father" and "Lord" in the new liturgy. Throughout the liturgy, however, "Lord" always means the Father, except where it explicitly says "Lord, Jesus Christ." In English, when we use the word "Lord," we usually mean Jesus, Our Lord. We therefore instinctively tend to interpret such phrases as "Lord, remember your Church" as referring to Jesus, rather than the Father. This ambiguous use of the word "Lord" leads to confusion, since at any particular point in the Eucharistic prayer it means that, in practice, we are unsure of whom we are talking to. This confusion is doubly compounded by the Eucharistic Acclamations 2, 3 and 4, which are addressed to Jesus. The 1st Acclamation avoids this, and also it is truly a "proclamation."

In spite of an opposite opinion held by some authorities, I think that the acclamations need to continue the direction of the Eucharistic prayer itself and ought to be addressed to the Father. The Aborginal liturgy, from the Melbourne Congress, gave us an example of a very simple acclamation addressed to the Father: "Father you are good." Normally, of course, the acclamation needs to contain the substance of the Christian proclamation: Christ has died, Christ is risen, Christ will come again.

Let us proclaim the mystery of Faith. To whom do we proclaim? First, to the Father, then to ourselves, the Church, and then to the world.

Keep in mind then that we are praying to the Father; and the sacred elements of bread and wine, which we hold in our hands, are the covenant sign by which we may demand of the Father that he fulfil his covenant for us.

There are some disappointing inadequacies in various parts of the new Eucharistic prayers. This is especially true of the way in which the sacred elements are variously referred to as "bread and wine," or "body and blood" or even "see the victim whose death has reconciled us to yourself." This is a distinct break with tradition. No Eucharistic prayer used by the Church has ever before referred to the sacramental elements by any words other than "bread and wine" or "our gifts," even after the Consecration. St. Paul's phrase remains our guide to orthodox wording here: "When we eat this bread and drink this cup we proclaim the death of the Lord until he comes." But this is not a matter merely of wording. It suggests that what we offer is the "Blessed Sacrament." Once more we are slipping from the realm of ritual (sacrament) into the area of mime.

Apart from the questions of theological language, there is something wrong with the new Eucharistic prayers, which makes them fail to hold the attention of the congregation; and here the disadvantages of liturgy composed-by-committees become blatant. No matter how hard people try, everyone seems to lose the thread, and becomes distracted. One recognises that we must not worry about distractions, and that real prayer absorbs a person so that one is often unaware of the detailed contents of the words. But such prayerful involvement is quite different from the distractedness so many experience at present. This, of course, partly derives from the sheer battering of words to which they are subjected, but it is also due to the sense that the Eucharistic prayers meander from one paragraph to the next, without much obvious connection between paragraphs.

One writer has pointed out that intercessions belong to the fourth category in the division of the elements of a Eucharistic prayer, that is, they are desirable but not necessary. Yet in Canon III, intercessions take up thirty-five percent of all the words used. Certainly this must be regarded as an example of ritual imbalance. Intercessions, which really belong in the prayers of the faithful, are tumbled into the middle of the Eucharistic prayer. Small wonder then if we cannot remember how the thing started, or if we have forgotten halfway through what the paragraph was saying.

Strictly speaking, the Eucharistic prayer is one paragraph from beginning to end. It is one statement, addressed to the Father, from the opening words of the Preface, through to the final doxology: "Through Him, with Him, in Him, all glory and honour is yours, almighty Father . . . ." Unfortunately it deviates so much that most of us, priests as well as people, do mentally stray.

The most successful corrective to this weakness is the use of repeated acclamations throughout the Eucharistic prayer, punctuating it, as in the Eucharistic prayer for children's Masses. Such an acclamation is repeated four or five times during the Canon. They provide a constant clue to keep us on target. A further selection of acclamations, for use throughout the Eucharistic liturgy, would probably be of more use than the extra Eucharistic prayers at present being composed.

At the same time, we must, for the sake of realism, remember that Eucharistic Prayer II, even when said slowly, takes only three minutes to recite. Obviously, then, the distraction and boredom people complain of at Mass is not due to the length of time taken. Neither, on the other hand, can the weaknesses be ascribed to the ritual actions. Somehow the texts will have to be allowed to mellow and be modified over the years. Yet it remains true that we now have a liturgy none of us could have thought possible twenty years ago. The ritual elements of the bread and the wine are beautifully high-lighted. Perhaps in time we may even get to the point of imitating St. Thomas, who always drank a full chalice of wine at Mass, knowing as he did that we need to have the experience of eating and drinking. This, of course, is also the advantage of using a more substantial type of unleavened bread.

Three or four of the decrees state that the bread used in the Mass should "look like bread, taste like bread and have the texture of bread." Also, since the Lord's command was "take and drink of this cup" more should be done to take advantage of the general law – that communion may be received under both species "whenever it is convenient, and can be done with dignity."

It is quite silly to argue about such minor things as the sign of peace, when the principal sacramental symbols of bread and wine are languishing in a shrivelled and petrified condition. The history of the sign of peace is quite obscure. One theory holds that this practice arose at the time when it was becoming common for people not to receive communion at Mass. The sign of peace was given as a substitute for receiving communion, to symbolise the union of the community in the Body of Christ, the Church. Of course, sharing in the one bread is the essential sacramental sign of that union. With such a doubtful origin, it would be well not to make the "sign of peace" the emblem of our enthusiasms and our liturgical campaigns.

We must learn to use the sacramental elements of bread and wine well. Learn to look at them, associating them, perhaps with the toast, certainly with the covenant – the symbolum of God's covenant with us in Christ. As we hold the host in our hands we recall the words "When we eat this bread and drink this cup, we proclaim his death until he comes . . . Father, remember Calvary." In time, the unsatisfactory elements of the text will iron themselves out. We will eventually know what is to be done; none of us really knows now. Ritual-by-committee will eventually be mellowed and its deficiencies set right by the instinct of the Church at prayer.

BIBLIOGRAPHY

TWELVE GENERAL WORKS ON
EUCHARIST AND LITURGY

ROGUET, A.M.
Holy Mass: approaches to the mystery. New Ed. Collegeville, Minn., Liturgical Press (1975)

DALMAIS, I.H.
Introduction to the liturgy. Baltimore, Helicon Press; London, G. Chapman (1961)

CRICHTON, JAMES DUNLOP
Christian celebration: The Mass. London, G. Chapman (1971)

POWERS, JOSEPH M.
Eucharistic theology. New York, Herder & Herder (1967) Bibliography.

LASH, NICHOLAS
His presence in the world: a study in eucharistic worship and theology. London, Sheed & Ward; Dayton, Pflaum Press (1968)

DEISS, LUCIEN
Early sources of the liturgy, London, G. Chapman (1967) Bibliography.

WINSTONE, HAROLD
Pastoral liturgy: a symposium edited by Harold Winstone. London, Collins (1975)

HELLWIG, MONIKA
The meaning of the sacraments. Dayton, Ohio, Pflaum (1972) Bibliography.

GELINEAU, JOSEPH
The liturgy today and tommorrow. London, Darton, Longman & Todd (1978)

YARNOLD, EDWARD
The study of liturgy. Edited by Cheslyn Jones, Geoffrey Wainwright, Edward Yarnold. London, SPCK (1978)

SCHILLEBEECKX, EDWARD
Christ the sacrament of encounter with God. New York & London, Sheed and Ward (1963)

SCHILLEBEECKX, EDWARD
The Eucharist. New York & London, Sheed & Ward (1968)

FOUR PRACTICAL GUIDES TO PLANNING

1. **HOVDA, ROBERT W.**
Strong, loving and wise: presiding in liturgy. Washington Liturgical Conference 78-38 (1976)

2. **HOVDA, ROBERT W.**
Dry bones; living worship guides to good liturgy. Washington, Liturgical Conference, 1973.
Includes bibliographical references

3. **MOSSI, JOHN P.**
Modern liturgy handbook: A study and planning guide for worship. Edited by John P. Mossi. New York, Paulist Press (1976)

4. **HOVDA, ROBERT W.**
There's no place like people: planning small group liturgies by Robert W. Hovda and Gabe Huck. 2d., Chicago, Argus Communications (1971)

THE LITURGY

CHAPTER II
Bishops' Committee on the Liturgy
Environment and Art in Catholic Worship
National Conference of Catholic Bishops 1978

DIVINE, GEORGE
Liturgical renewal: an agonising reappraisal. New York, Alba House (1973)

RITUAL

CHAPTER III

SHAUGHNESSY, JAMES D.
The roots of ritual. Grand Rapids, Eerdmans (1973)

MITCHELL, LEONEL L.
The meaning of ritual. New York, Paulist Press (1977)

HITCHCOCK, JAMES
The recovery of the sacred. New York, Seabury Press (1974) Bibliographical footnotes

CHAPTER VIII

HARRISON, G. B. and McCABE, JOHN
Proclaiming the Word. Pueblo Publishing Company, New York (1976) A Handbook for Church Speaking

MUSIC

CHAPTER V

Music in Catholic worship. Washington, Bishops' Committee on the liturgy, 1972

DEISS, LUCIEN
Spirit and song of the new liturgy. Cincinnati, World Library of Sacred Music (1970)   Bibliographical notes.

DEVOTION

CHAPTER VI

GALLEN, JOHN
CHRISTIANS at prayer. Edited by John Gallen. London, University of Notre Dame Press (1977)

CHAPTER VII

MURPHY-O'CONNOR, JEROME OP
Becoming Human Together. Michael Glazier, Inc.

MADE, not born: new perspectives on Christian initiation and the catechumenate. Notre Dame, University of Notre Dame Press (1976) 183p. 24cm. (Papers presented at a symposium sponsored by the Murphy Center for Liturgical Research) Bibliography.